Training Your Dog To Win Obedience Titles

by CURT MORSELL

Photographs by James Harrelson, Sr.

FIRST EDITION

HOWELL
BOOK HOUSE
New York

HOWELL BOOK HOUSE
Macmillan Publishing Company
866 Third Avenue, New York, NY 10022
Collier Macmillan Canada, Inc.

Library of Congress Catalog Card No. 76-215-86
ISBN 0-87605-674-5

Macmillan books are available at special discounts for bulk purchases
for sales promotions, premiums, fund-raising, or educational use.
For details, contact:

      Special Sales Director
      Macmillan Publishing Company
      866 Third Avenue
      New York, NY 10022

10 9 8

Printed in the United States of America

Thunder and two of his young offspring practice the Utility stand.

The author.

Dog Writers' Association
of America

presents this certificate of award to

Curt Morsell

in "Front and Finish"
National Bulletin ~ Best Series

_____
PRESIDENT

_____
SECRETARY

_____
CONTEST CHAIRMAN

February 9, 1975
DATE

Foreword

MUCH OF THE MATERIAL in this book first ap-
peared, as a monthly series, in *Front & Finish, The Dog Trainers'
News* under the title "The Education of an Obedience Trial Dog." It
was selected as the best series in a national publication by the Dog
Writers' Association of America in 1975.

The book is a detailed, step-by-step account of the training of a dog
for obedience trial competition. However, it is more than just another
dog training manual. It is the story of a teenage youngster and his best
pal — his dog. It tells of their trials and tribulations, their successes
and their failures.

Written by Curt Morsell, one of America's foremost professional
dog trainers, this book is ideal for those who are interested in training
and showing their dogs in obedience trials. But whether you're aiming
your dog toward Obedience degrees, or simply toward making him an
obedient, well-mannered pet, the clearly-illustrated techniques shown
here are sure to make the training a lot easier — and a lot more fun —
for you.

Mr. Morsell's qualifications are many. In addition to being a professional trainer with twenty-five years experience in dog obedience
work, he is an AKC-approved obedience trial judge, an author of nu-
merous articles on dog training, and was for a number of years the obedience editor of *Dog World* magazine.

> — *Elsworth S. Howell*
> *Publisher*

MY THANKS to John Richard Young, the noted horse and dog trainer, nationally-known author, and true friend. Without Jack Young's invaluable criticism, suggestions, and assistance this book would not have been possible.

Thanks, too, to "my severest critic", the gal who spent countless hours typing and editing the original manuscript — my wife, Sally.

I also wish to acknowledge the assistance and helpful suggestions contributed by the instructors' staff of my training school. These skilled and dedicated dog trainers include: Diane Coker, Diane Hodges, Jan Kren, Jean Marshall, Louise Richards, Rudy Richards and Ted Thomas.

— *Curt Morsell*

Contents

PART I
NOVICE TRAINING

PART II
OPEN TRAINING

PART III
UTILITY TRAINING

Preface

A NUMBER of people have asked me, since I began writing this book, why I am willing to share my training "secrets" with others, particularly since I am still very active in exhibiting my own dogs in trials. "Why," one woman asked, "are you willing to give tips to others that just might mean that their dogs will beat yours in a trial?"

The answer is simple.

First, the training procedures outlined in this book are not "my secrets." With very few exceptions, the methods we used in training Thunder are standard training techniques, employed by many obedience instructors throughout the United States.

The purpose of this book is not to introduce a "new and revolutionary" training method. Rather, the purpose is to demonstrate that anyone, following the procedures described, can train his dog for obedience competition — and do well!

If one exhibitor learns something from the book that helps him to earn a leg toward an obedience title, instead of a non-qualifying score, it will have served its purpose.

POPULAR DOGS

"200" CLUB"

CERTIFICATE OF MERIT

Signifying that

CURT'S BROWNBERRY BELLE

Scored 200 points at an American Kennel Club
Licenced Obedience Trial

Show NORTH SHORE DOG TRAINING CLUB   Date May 17, 1964

Judge Miss H. Kusler   Owner's Name Curtis B. Morsell, Jr.

Editor, POPULAR DOGS

Award of Canine Distinction

To Whom It may Concern -- Greetings:

THERE IS HEREBY ISSUED by Dog World Magazine, thru
the action of its Committee of Awards, this AWARD OF
CANINE DISTINCTION to:

Name of Dog   CURT'S BROWNBERRY BELLE

Breed   Standard Poodle   **Sex**   Bitch

Owned by

Curtis B. Morsell, Jr.
5249 North Diversey Blvd.
Milwaukee, Wisconsin 53217

For the following outstanding, meritorious and most note-
worthy accomplishment in the field of dogs, dog breeding
and showing, to wit:

Won her UD Degree in her first three trials
with the following high scores--

9/5/64, Lombard, Illinois--198
9/12/64, Cambridge, Wisconsin--199
9/13/64, Manitowoc, Wisconsin--196 1/2

In public recognition of this worthy record, the Committee has
enrolled the award as a permanent record in its ALBUM OF GREAT
DOGS OF THE PAST AND PRESENT, this   19th
day of   October   1964 , at Chicago, state of
Illinois, United States of America, and does hereby certify the award
with its signatures.

COMMITTEE OF CANINE AWARDS

By _____ CHAIRMAN

Attest:
Leslie Lynn
Secretary of Committee
and Custodian of Records

Why Obedience Training?

A NUMBER of articles have been written recently criticizing present-day obedience training practices, as well as AKC obedience trials. One well-known conformation judge, for example, stated in a national publication that today's obedience training is "impractical." He stated further that modern obedience trials are "uninteresting."

On behalf of the many thousands of obedience enthusiasts throughout the United States, I must take exception to these charges.

The benefits of training a dog in obedience are many. To say that obedience training is impractical, or of little value, is nonsense.

Typical of the reaction of the average dog owner who has given his dog obedience training were the remarks made to me recently by a middle-aged woman whose dog I judged at an obedience match. It was her first experience in a trial. She told me that she didn't really care if her dog passed. "I am amazed," she said, "that he has learned as much as he has." She was happy just having a dog that was well-enough trained to compete in an obedience trial.

"Six months ago," she went on, "George was wild and uncontrollable. I couldn't do a thing with him. Despite the fact that I loved him I was on the verge of getting rid of him when a friend suggested I take him to an obedience training class. Now, just three months later, George is not only a well-behaved pet that I can be proud of, but here I am actually showing him in an obedience match."

This is the sort of tribute one regularly hears from people who have taken their dogs through formal obedience training. It is indisputable evidence that present-day training techniques are not only practical, they are *successful*.

Today's training procedures are the result of years of study and constant improvement by experts in the field. They are designed to produce dogs that are better equipped than ever before to take their places in our modern urban society. As in everything else, there are exceptions, of course, but the great majority of obedience trained dogs are consistently well-mannered. They are dogdom's most effective goodwill ambassadors to the public at large.

In addition to the obvious advantages of training a dog in obedience, there are also a number of other, less tangible benefits which are nonetheless real. One gratifying reward of joining a training class, for example, is that many friendships are developed among people of similar interests. Important, too, is the fact that dogs love training. If you work with your dog regularly he looks forward eagerly to these periods with his beloved "man god."

With respect to the complaint that AKC obedience trials are uninteresting for spectators, suffice it to say that a bridge tournament or chess match is uninteresting if the viewer doesn't understand the intricacies of the game. To a real obedience buff, however, there is nothing more interesting than watching a sharp dog perform in the Utility ring, or witnessing a run-off between two precise, smooth-working dogs, quick and eager to obey.

In short, to those who appreciate well-trained dogs, and who recognize the many hours that go into their training, obedience trial competition is not only interesting, it is one of the most fascinating sports there is.

Which is the "Best" Breed for Obedience Competition?

From what I have observed over the years, I am convinced that there is no one breed that is smarter, or a better trial dog, than others. I own a Standard Poodle and a German Shepherd Dog. Both of these breeds make good obedience trial dogs, generally speaking. However, I have also trained dogs of other breeds that turned out to be excellent trial dogs. In my opinion, the most important thing is not the breed; it is the intelligence and trainability of the individual dog, plus the ability and dedication of his trainer.

Certainly there are some breeds that exhibit a greater tendency to be "bull headed" or slower learners than others. However, while this may be an inherited characteristic of the breed it does not necessarily follow that they cannot become excellent obedience workers. Several of the finest trial dogs I have seen, for example, were Boxers — a breed considered by some to be headstrong and almost impossible to train for obedience work. Moreover, one of the best obedience dogs campaigning in our area a few years ago was a Malamute, another breed many people believe to be one of the most difficult to train.

It is true that we see more Poodles and Shepherds in obedience trials today than any other breeds. However, this is not only due to the fact that they are very trainable, it is also due to the simple fact that there are more of them around — they rank first and second in number of registrations by a wide margin. Obviously, with the preponderance of entrants coming from these two breeds they should by the law of averages walk off with the lion's share of the honors in obedience trials. One doesn't have to look too far, however, to find a number of exceptions to the trend.

An analysis I made of the published trial results throughout the country during a recent month showed that dogs of *fifty-one* different breeds placed in the ribbons in their obedience classes during the month! This is a remarkable representation of the dog world. The top dogs ranged all the way from little Chihuahuas and Papillons to Great Danes and Saint Bernards. The list of winners included such uncommon obedience competitors as Rhodesian Ridgebacks, Italian Greyhounds, Pulik, Afghans, Vizlas, and Minpins.

Certainly this is convincing evidence that almost every breed of dog is capable of doing well in obedience competition. The most important thing is the intelligence and trainability of the individual dog.

Another factor which I should mention here is that in addition to being reasonably intelligent and trainable, a good obedience trial dog must be structurally sound.

I don't mean that their owners should be discouraged from training dogs with a physical disability, such as malformed hip joints or incorrect shoulder angulation. Such dogs can derive a lot of benefit from the Basic and Novice obedience classes. However, a dog with hip dysplasia or some other form of subluxation will usually tire faster than his normal classmates during training sessions, even though he may not limp or show any other visible signs of discomfort. The result is that his concentration span will be shorter. In addition, if it is physically painful for him the dog will resent his training. He will more than likely become stubborn and uncorporative. Unfortunately, when this happens, if the owner is not aware of his dog's disability (which is frequently the situation) he will conclude that his dog is hard-headed, or mentally retarded, which is not true. Consequently, even in the beginning classes it is important that a dog be physically sound if he is to be a good obedience worker.

In the more advanced obedience classes a dog is at an even greater disadvantage if he is not structurally sound. A dog with poorly-formed hips or faulty front assembly, for example, will frequently have trouble with the jumping exercises in the Open and Utility classes. In competition, most breeds must jump one and a half times their own height at the shoulder, which is no mean feat even for sound dog.

In summary, if you want a dog that will be a good obedience worker, the breed is not as important as the mental *and* physical soundness of the individual dog.

The Ten Commandments of Obedience Training

1. PRAISE YOUR DOG when he performs an exercise correctly. This is what your dog is working for—your praise!

2. CORRECT YOUR DOG *FIRMLY* when he fails to perform an exercise properly—if you are sure he *understands* what is expected of him.

3. THINK LIKE A DOG. Put yourself in your dog's shoes, and train him accordingly. Don't punish your dog for performing an exercise incorrectly when it is likely that he doesn't understand what you want.

4. HAVE PATIENCE. If you lose your temper you'll do more harm than good; put your leash away until tomorrow.

5. DO YOUR HOMEWORK. Your instructors can show you *how* to train your dog—but the important part is up to you.

6. GET YOUR DOG'S ATTENTION while working with him. Talk to him, or use the leash to keep him attentive. Use tidbits or other training aids if necessary.

7. DON'T CALL YOUR DOG TO YOU AND THEN PUNISH HIM! He will think he is being punished for *coming.*

8. CONSISTENCY IS THE NAME OF THE GAME. Your dog will not learn right from wrong if you allow him to do something one day and then punish him the next day for doing the same thing (jumping on the couch, etc.)

9. BE YOUR DOG'S *MASTER.* Don't *ask* your dog to do something—*tell* him. A dog will happily obey a master he respects. Moreover, dogs equate respect with love. The firmer you are with your dog the more he will love you. (I said "firm," not "cruel.")

10. PRACTICE EVERY DAY, rain or shine. Success in dog training is 90% practice.

Part 1

NOVICE TRAINING

Thunder meets his new family.

Thunder Finds
a New Home

SCANNING the classified ad section of the Sunday paper, I noted that a litter of eleven-week-old German Shepherd pups was for sale at a nearby breeder's. I decided right then that what we needed around our apartment was another dog.

When we moved to Savannah from Wisconsin several months earlier I found that there was no dog training club or school in the area. So I was forced to organize my own — thus the birth of The Savannah Dog Training School. However, teaching other people to train their dogs gave me the bug to start training another pup of my own, since Clancy, our Standard Poodle, was eleven years old and no longer able to compete in obedience trials.

For fear Sally, my wife, would find out what I was up to (for some odd reason she thinks one big dog in an apartment is enough) I stole out of the house before she was up. I drove over to take a look at the litter.

There were ten pups. Most were black and tan. I prefer this color, but a large-boned, quick-moving gray male caught my eye — it was love at first sight. He was the one I had to have.

I learned that this pup already had a name — Thunder. They had named him this several weeks earlier when a sudden thunderstorm broke and the breeder's children quickly rounded up the pups and took them inside; all, that is, except one inquisitive pup who was off exploring a neighbor's flower garden — the gray male. As a result he was out in the storm for several hours. From that time on he was known as Thunder. I liked the name and saw no reason for changing it. I decided to make his official registered name *Thunder Over Dixie*.

Sally welcomed the pup with something less than unbounded enthusiasm, but Thunder soon settled down and within a few days was completely at home. In fact, exhibiting the typical temperament of a good Shepherd, within a week he was our self-appointed protector — making certain no strange dogs wandered into our yard. It was funny to see this three months old squirt rush out after dogs four times his size, growling and barking like a real big shot. If nothing else, it was obvious Thunder didn't lack courage.

With people, however, Thunder was convinced everybody loved him, displaying a very affectionate and gentle disposition. He even won Sally's heart within a few days. More than once I caught her saving choice tidbits from our dinner for "the little gray rat," as she fondly called him.

The only member of the family that did not take to Thunder was old Clancy. At eleven, Clancy was jealous of this young intruder. He was in no mood for horseplay despite Thunder's repeated attempts to engage him in mock battles or ear-biting contests. With a growl that obviously meant "Beat it, you little pest," Clancy would turn his back and stalk away every time the pup came near him. It was several weeks before the old Poodle fully accepted Thunder.

When the pup reached three and a half months of age I decided to start his obedience training. However, before introducing a dog to the leash, in my opinion, there is something far more critical he must learn.

In order to have a really happy, obedient dog, whether you ever intend to enter him in obedience trials or not, you have to teach him that you are Almighty, the Dispenser of All Good, the Giver of All Goodies. In short, you teach him that it is a joy to come when you call him. You are the one safe refuge in all the world. If he comes to your call, or runs to you without being called, you should tidbit and/or caress him. You will never punish him if he comes when called. Get this idea into his head from the very beginning. It is the foundation upon which the training of all good-working obedience trial dogs is based.

Once this was accomplished Thunder was ready to start his formal training.

As an AKC obedience judge, instructor, and obedience enthusiast for over twenty-five years, if there is one thing I've learned it's that no two dogs are alike. Many times you have to adapt your training methods somewhat to the particular dog you're training. A number or years ago, for example, when I trained and showed my brown Standard Poodle bitch, Curt's Brownberry Belle, U.D., to a record that had never before been accomplished, winning the *Dog World* Award (all scores over 195) in all three classes — Novice, Open, and Utility — I had to stick strictly to praise and very gentle corrections in her early training. I never used a prong training collar, as she was too sensitive. She

Thunder Over Dixie at 11 weeks.

would go into a shell if I got rough with her. With Thunder, however, I found that the prong collar, or "spike collar" as it is sometimes called, was an excellent training aid. It was obvious from the start that Thunder had a will of his own.

Now I know that many who read this will throw up their hands and say, "That brute, he's cruel!" However, the so-called "spike" collar bears a misleading name, for the "spikes" are nothing more than blunt-ended fingers which will exert momentary pressure on the dog's neck when the leash is jerked. Moreover, there is an automatic stop on the collar which prevents it from being pulled so tight that it will choke the dog, as the more popular slip chain or "choker chain" collar will do. Prong collars are not allowed in obedience rings, but for my money one can be a definite aid with a dog that is a little stubborn in his early schooling.

Proper way to place slip chain collar on dog. (Free, or "live" ring should be on the dog's right.)

Thunder heeling on leash with his new handler. (Note the slack in the leash — to avoid a possible penalty for "guiding.")

Heeling on Leash

TRIAL REQUIREMENTS:
On the judge's order, "Forward," the handler may give a vocal command or hand signal to Heel. He will walk in a natural manner, with the dog at his left side — with the leash slack. The judge will give the orders, "Forward," "Halt," "Right Turn," "Left Turn," "About Turn," "Fast," "Slow," and "Normal." These orders may be given in any sequence. The "About Turn" shall be a right about turn in all cases. It is permissible after each Halt, before moving again, for the handler to give the command or signal to Heel.

In the "Figure 8" portion of the exercise the handler and dog shall walk around and between two persons who are positioned about eight feet apart.

FAULTS:
Using the leash to guide the dog; failure of the dog or handler to change pace noticeably for "Slow" or "Fast;" forging or lagging while heeling; crowding or heeling wide; crooked sits.

THE FIRST EXERCISE to teach a future obedience trial dog is to heel on leash. Unlike some other trainers, I believe in "baiting" a dog (that is, offering him tidbits.) With a young dog it will make him want to keep up with you while heeling, rather than your having to drag him along. If baiting is used occasionally all through your dog's training it will help keep his eyes glued on you, instead of having him looking about, paying little or no attention to you. As a judge, there is nothing more impressive to me than a dog that never takes his eyes off his handler. If it takes "baiting" to achieve this with your dog then I'm all for it! Remember, however, that you're *never* allowed to take food into the ring in an obedience trial.

When heeling your dog you want his shoulder right next to your left leg, but without his touching or crowding you. I personally prefer a "close-working" dog that stays within three or four inches of his handler's leg.

For the first few days of his training I kept Thunder on a very short, taut leash so that he had to stay right next to my leg, despite his occasional attempts to pull away or to fight the leash. I used quick, firm jerks on the leash (rather than a continuous pulling or tugging), and with the help of a few tidbits plus a lot of praise, Thunder gradually began to get it through his head that the command "Heel" meant walking along right next to me. After about four days Thunder was heeling well enough so that I was able to loosen the leash somewhat, thus giving him a chance to forge ahead of me or to lag behind.

To cure Thunder of forging I grasped the leash in my left hand and jerked him back while simultaneously repeating the command, "Heel, heel;" adding praise when he was again at my side. Surprisingly, it took only one day to break him of forging. I was very fortunate in this respect. With dogs that are habitual "forgers" I recommend abrupt, unexpected turns, especially left turns, and frequent quick about turns. These, in addition to sharp jerks on the leash, are usually effective in slowing down a "forger."

Lagging was a different story. Thunder had a definite tendency to lag. It was here that I had a problem.

In order to cure Thunder of lagging all of our early heeling sessions were done in "double time;" that is, I worked him at a fast trot with a lot of quick turns and about turns in an attempt to get him moving faster. The quick turns also helped to keep his attention focused on me. He never knew when I would make a sudden turn, and if he wasn't paying attention it resulted in an unpleasant jerk on the leash. I knew that unless I could correct this problem in the early stages of his training, lagging could plague Thunder's work throughout his obedience career.

If there is one thing I admire in an obedience ring, it's a quick-moving dog that sticks to his handler like a burr on a Collie regardless of how fast the handler moves. I was determined Thunder was not going to be a lagger, whatever other faults he might develop, even if it meant a coronary for his overweight and out-of-condition handler.

Lagging. Short, sharp forward jerks on the leash, plus a lot of "double time" heeling, will cure.

Forging. Jerk back on the leash, together with a lot of sudden about turns. And *praise* your dog when he is in the proper heel position.

With respect to the Figure 8, during your practice sessions it is not always possible to find two people to act as "posts." In lieu of human posts, however, I have found that two lawn chairs or other convenient obstacles spaced about eight feet apart serve as an adequate substitute, although human "posts" are better in order to teach your dog not to sniff or shy from the posts.

In conjunction with his heeling lessons I also introduced Thunder to the automatic sit every time I came to a halt. To achieve this, as soon as I stopped I pulled up hard on the leash with my right hand while simultaneously pushing down on his hindquarters with my left hand.

It took only about four days for Thunder to learn the automatic sit, although his sits were typically uncoordinated puppy sits, with his rear legs flopped out in all directions. Although I corrected his position every time he sat crooked, at that stage I was not too concerned with the straightness of his sits. A young pup is just not physically capable of perfect sits.

When Thunder reached five months of age our son Fred, who had just turned thirteen, asked if he could have Thunder for his own. He also wanted to take over Thunder's training.

I was delighted. Not only was I pleased to have Fred show an interest in obedience training as a hobby, but for all practical purposes Thunder was already Fred's dog. Right from the first Thunder had adopted Fred as his favorite member of the family. They romped together, played together, and even slept together. Many mornings when I went into his bedroom to wake Fred for school I found the "little gray rat" (who now weighed close to 60 pounds) asleep on the bed alongside of Fred — with his head on the pillow right next to his young master's.

To say that they were real pals would be an understatement. It was as touching a case of genuine love between a boy and his dog as I have ever seen. It was right out of an Albert Payson Terhune novel.

There was another reason I was pleased that Fred wished to take over Thunder's training. I was about to start a new Beginners' class at my training school. This gave me an opportunity to get Thunder into the course, with Fred handling him, while I conducted the class.

With his basic training already behind him, Thunder was ahead of his classmates, of course. In his daily training sessions at home the pup was performing all of the Novice exercises fairly well, in addition to having started retrieving and jumping (as I will get into in more detail in Part II, Open Training). What Thunder needed,

The automatic sit —
Step One: Pull upward on leash with right hand while simultaneously pushing down on dog's hindquarters with left hand.

Step Two: The dog should be seated right next to handler's left leg, and in a straight position.

A perfect sit, front view.

however, was exposure to other dogs and people. This is essential in order to prepare a dog for the noise, swarms of people, and general chaos that usually characterize an obedience trial. Now he had the opportunity to work with other dogs and people around.

In addition, Thunder had developed a bad habit that needed correction. In my efforts to ensure that Thunder would be a close-working dog I had trained him to stay close against my left leg while heeling. As a result he was crowding me, and bumping me on the left turns. The lazy loafer also liked to rest against my leg when he was sitting at the heel position.

To cure Thunder of crowding we resorted to an old gimmick. I had Fred take Thunder's prong collar off and put it around his own leg, with the prongs pointed out. Thus every time Thunder got too close to Fred's leg he would bump against the prongs. Using this means it took less than a week to cure Thunder of crowding.

In teaching Fred to be a polished handler there were some "finer points" he had to learn. Regardless of his dog's performance in his first trial (which is beyond the handler's control once he steps into the ring) I wanted Fred to look like a knowledgeable handler. Judges don't make allowances for the age or inexperience of a handler. They can't. Each handler and dog must be judged by the same standard.

One of the important things a handler must learn, for example, is where to position his hands while heeling.

In the old days many handlers, particularly those with big dogs, placed their left hands behind their backs while heeling. This was to ensure that their hands would not strike or distract the dogs. However, the AKC Obedience Regulations now specifically state that the handler must walk in a "natural manner," which has been officially interpreted as precluding a handler from walking with one hand behind his back. The handler *may*, however, walk with his left hand in *front*, at the waist, if held naturally and giving no aid to the dog.

Another point on which the revised regulations are vague concerns the dog who heels with his head turned so that he can keep his eyes on his handler. A few judges take the position that the dog should face perfectly straight ahead. However, the consensus of most judges and obedience authorities is that a dog working with his head turned should not be penalized. Rather, it is their feeling that this degree of attentiveness should be *encouraged!*

In the Heel on Leash exercise there are a number of errors that are repeatedly committed by inexperienced handlers. One of the most common is guiding the dog with the leash. In this exercise the leash should remain slack. Some handlers apparently believe, however, that they can surreptitiously prevent their dogs from lagging by shortening the leash. Unfortunately, this ploy seldom escapes the judge's notice. The result is that the handler usually loses more points for guiding with the leash than his dog would have lost for a little lagging.

In both the Heel On Leash and Heel Free exercises some handlers are also guilty of making their turns too sharply, or so-called military turns. This is not only unnecessary, it makes it very difficult for the dog to get out of the way on the left turns. Too sharp a right turn, on the other hand, is likely to catch the dog unaware and cause him to lag. The perfect turn is neither too sharp, nor too roundabout; rather, it is a natural turn. Similarly, the about turn should also be a natural movement, not the dipsy-doodle or other exaggerated dance steps sometimes seen in the ring.

A pet peeve when I was active as an obedience trial judge was that some handlers did not change their pace enough on the "slow" and "fast" orders while heeling. I don't know why some people refuse to make a definite change of pace in this exercise. Instead, they merely shift gears slightly and go right on walking almost exactly as before. The object of this part of the exercise is to determine whether the dog will immediately adapt his pace to that of his handler. Under the AKC regulations the refusal of a handler to make a definite change in speed should be substantially penalized.

Another common failing in the heeling exercises is that many handlers stop too abruptly on the "Halt" order. This is an error Fred frequently made in his early training sessions with Thunder. The result is that the handler catches his dog by surprise and the dog inadvertently forges ahead when the handler stops, which calls for a deduction even though the dog may correct himself and back into the proper sitting position.

Most judges will allow one or two steps after the "Halt" order. The experienced handler will take advantage of this to slow more smoothly and gradually to a stop, thereby giving his dog advance warning and reducing the chances of his forging.

This legitimate "trick" can be very important in avoiding the loss of crucial points in an obedience trial. In fact, it can sometimes mean the difference between placing in the ribbons or being an "also-ran." Consequently, Fred and I worked long and hard at perfecting this phase of his heeling technique. It was clearly reflected in Thunder's improved performance.

Question: You are the judge in the Novice ring. As the handler enters the ring and positions himself to start the "Heel On Leash" exercise, you notice that he is holding the leash with both hands. He has the end of the leash in his right hand, and his left hand is also grasping the leash about 10 or 12 inches from the end. What, if anything, do you do?

Answer: You do nothing. The AKC regulations permit the leash to be held in either hand, or *both hands.* Most experienced handlers prefer to carry the leash in their right hands, to ensure sufficient slack in the leash. Thus they minimize the possibility of a penalty for guiding their dogs with the leashes.

The "two hands on the leash" situation arose in my ring at a trial some time ago, and another exhibitor in the class was quite upset when she learned I had not penalized the other handler for this "obvious violation" of the regulations.

This points up a situation that has bothered me for some time. In recent years it seems that more and more exhibitors, particularly in the Novice A class, are entering trials without ever having read the AKC regulations pertaining to their class. This is inexcusable, especially since copies of the regulations may be readily obtained from the AKC. (Single copies of the booklet "Obedience Regulations" will be mailed without charge on individual request to the American Kennel Club, 51 Madison Avenue, New York, N.Y. 10010. If ordered in quantity, there is a charge of 15 cents per booklet.)

Stand for Examination

TRIAL REQUIREMENTS:
On the judge's order to "Stand your dog for examination" the handler will stand his dog, off leash, walk at least six feet away, and turn and face his dog. The judge will examine the dog by touching its head, body, and hindquarters. On the order "Back to your dog" the handler must walk around behind his dog to the heel position.

FAULTS:
Faults resulting in a score of zero for the exercise include the dog showing resentment, shyness, growling, snapping, or sitting or moving away from the spot where it was left before the examination is completed. Deductions shall be made for a dog that moves its feet, sits, or moves away after the examination is completed.

WITH MOST DOGS of normal intelligence the Stand for Exam is a relatively easy exercise to learn.

The principal exceptions are those dogs, usually members of the smaller breeds, that are so exuberant and frisky that they can't control themselves. They *have* to move forward to greet the judge. With these lovable little tykes stern correction every time the dog so much as moves a paw, together with practice and *more* practice, is the only solution.

Another type of dog that presents a problem in the Stand for Exam is the shy or timid dog. These dogs frequently back away at the approach of the judge, or during his examination.

Raising a "biter's" front feet off the ground eliminates his ability to lunge forward, and minimizes his power.

To cure a timid dog have someone other than yourself, or a member of your family, examine the dog during your practice sessions whenever possible. All the while the "stranger" is examining him, talk to the dog in soft, reassuring tones. Tell him what a good dog he is, that there is nothing to fear. This, together with practice over a period of weeks, will eventually produce a dog that is steady on the Stand for Exam.

In my training class the type of dog I have the most trouble with in this exercise is the aggressive dog — the dog that would just as soon take a chunk out of your arm as look at you. There are many reasons why a dog is a "biter," be it heredity or environment. I won't get into a discussion of the various causes here. It is an unfortunate fact, however, that a small percentage of dogs are confirmed biters by the time they are enrolled in an obedience training class.

The cure I use for combating a habitual biter is to have it out with him right at the start. He *has* to be taught who is boss!

With the dog wearing a prong collar, and his handler holding him on a taut leash, I approach the dog. I always wear welder's gloves when dealing with a biter (my mother didn't raise any fools). If the dog growls or lunges at me, I have his handler jerk upward and rearward on the leash while simultaneously commanding, "NO!" Pulling up on the leash raises the dog's front end off the ground, where he is virtually powerless. At the same time I smack him under the jaw.

Usually only a few of these lessons are required. Ordinarily it isn't long before I can approach and examine the dog without incident; or, if the dog should snap or growl, a sharp "No!" from his handler will immediately make him stop. In those instances where the dog shows no signs of becoming less antagonistic after several weeks of training I usually advise the owner to have the dog disposed of. The dog is a menace to society. Sooner or later he will seriously injure someone, perhaps a child.

It may sound heartless to tell an owner that he should get rid of his beloved pet. However, with so many good dogs available, it just isn't sensible to keep a dog with a bad temperament. It not only could result in tragedy, as well as considerable medical and legal expenses for the owner, but it reflects badly on all dogdom.

It took Thunder about four weeks before he was fairly steady on the Stand for Exam.

Starting when the pup was five months old, Fred first had Thunder sit at the heel position. He then pulled forward on the leash while repeating the command, "Stand, stand." When Thunder was in the standing position Fred praised him and stroked his side. Occasionally the pup would start to sit but Fred quickly positioned his left foot under Thunder's stomach, with his toe pointed up. (See photo.) If the dog tried to sit, Fred's toe prodded him gently in the belly. With the Toy

The Stand for Exam, Step One: "S-t-a-n-d." (Note handler's left foot under the dog's stomach, to prevent him from sitting.)

Step Two: Walk out to end of leash, turn and face your dog.

Step Three: Have "stranger" examine dog.

Return to your dog around the *right* side.

In a trial, remain standing next to your dog until the judge's order, "Exercise finished."

breeds, of course, it is not possible to place your foot under the dog with your toe pointed up, but you can still position your foot beneath the dog — thus making it difficult for him to sit.

Within a week Thunder was reliable enough on the stand so that Fred could give him the "Stay" command and move out to the end of the leash. Once this was accomplished, we had a "judge" approach Thunder and examine him. At first he wagged his tail and moved several steps toward the judge. However, a stern reprimand by both Fred and the "judge" eventually convinced Thunder that moving from his original position was *verboten*.

Naturally Thunder occasionally "goofed", but by the time he was six months old he was fairly reliable. At this point Fred took the leash off. Happily, this did not effect Thunder's performance of the exercise. Further, by this time he was standing in response to a hand signal simulating a pulling forward of the leash — not unlike the sweeping, horizontal swing of the hand I use in the Utility signal exercise.

When he was about seven months old, for some reason Thunder became less dependable on the Stand for Exam. He reverted to his earlier habit of moving forward to investigate the stranger, particularly if it was a man. To correct this situation I had Fred give Thunder a good sharp "NO!" command every time he moved. This, together with a lot of practice with different "judges" soon cured the problem. (I'm afraid we were becoming a nuisance to our neighbors, whose aid we were constantly enlisting as "judges").

When a dog moves on the Stand for Exam exercise I don't believe in having the handler hit the dog. If he does, the dog is apt to shy or cower from the judge, thinking he is going to get smacked. Moreover, on the judge's order, "Back to your dog," the dog might believe his handler is returning to hit him, and move away. In the first case the dog receives a big fat zero for the exercise, of course, and even if he doesn't move until his handler is returning the dog will lose valuable points.

———————————

Question: In the Stand for Exam is it permissible to physically handle and pose your dog prior to giving him the "Stay" command and/or signal?

Answer: Yes. The exercise begins with the "Stay" command — except for such things as rough treatment of the dog by its handler, or active resistance by the dog to its handler's attempts to make him stand. In the latter situation the dog is considered out of control, which he may never be — even between exercises.

The Heel Free Exercise

TRIAL REQUIREMENTS:
This exercise shall be executed in the same manner as the Heel On Leash except that the dog is off leash, and the Figure 8 is omitted.

FAULTS:
Forging or lagging; crowding or heeling wide; crooked sits; failure of the dog or handler to change pace noticeably on the "Slow" or "Fast" orders.

IN MY OPINION, teaching the average dog to heel off leash is not as difficult as some professional trainers would have you believe.

In my Beginners' classes I start the dogs heeling off leash after only four weeks of training. This is in contrast to the theory advocated by many of my colleagues who won't even consider having a dog attempt to heel off leash until the dog has been in training at least six months. However, the method I use has proven successful, at least with the great majority of dogs in my training classes. At this writing, for example, in the past month my students have brought back five first places in trials around the Southeast, several with dogs that have been in training for less than five months.

It is my belief that after a dog has been heeling on leash for a month he should be doing fairly well. I have seen too many pups only three or four months old heeling beautifully on leash after only several weeks' practice not to be convinced that dogs are capable of absorbing a lot more training, and at a faster pace, than most of us think. Unfortunate-

Drop the leash, while heeling. If your dog starts to "break" quickly step on the end of the leash.

Wrapping leash loosely around your dog's neck will usually make him think he is still under your control.

ly, most of our present-day training classes are geared to the slower-learners in the class. I feel this is a mistake.

Once a dog is heeling well on leash it is usually a relatively easy transition to working him off leash. With most dogs I have found that when you unsnap the leash and order, "Heel," the dog will perform almost as well as he does on leash. Of course, when doing about turns and right turns, where the dog is apt to lag a little, a lot of vocal encouragement, leg-slapping, and tasty tidbits are helpful. If your dog has a serious problem with lagging or forging, immediately put the leash back on him and do some "double time" heeling, with quick, abrupt turns — preferably using the prong training collar. Then try it again off leash.

Initially, just a minute or so of off-leash heeling is sufficient. Gradually increase the duration, day-by-day. Above all, remember to praise and/or treat your dog for a job well done.

The type of dog that presents the greatest problem in this exercise is the dog that breaks and takes off for the wide blue yonder once his leash is removed. For these rambunctious rascals I use either of two methods in teaching them to heel free.

If your dog is one of those, "Ha, ha, you can't catch me now!" wise guys the minute he knows the leash is off, don't unsnap it from his collar. Merely let him drag the leash along beside him. Ordinarily the dog will still feel he is under your control. He will not try to escape. If he does start to take off, you have to use some fast footwork to step on the end of the leash before the dog gets away (if necessary use a long thin nylon cord instead of a leash). The sudden, and painful, jerk on his collar will make him think twice before trying that trick again.

Once your dog has become fairly dependable at heeling while dragging the leash, wrap the leash loosely around his neck. In most instances he will still feel that he is under your power. He will behave accordingly. Eventually, usually in less than two weeks, you should be able to take the leash off. If your dog has an occasional lapse, go right back to the method you used in the beginning — having him drag the leash. In a short time his "lapses" will become less frequent, and, eventually, you will have a dependable off-leash worker.

The other method I use to cure a dog from "breaking" when working off leash is the use of the so-called throw chain (many trainers use a slip chain collar). Most dogs hate to have something thrown at them. As a result, if your dog starts to break, yell "NO!" and have something to throw at him (I have found that in lieu of a chain, just throwing the leash at the dog works equally well). Up until this point your dog had always thought that when he got more than six or seven feet away from you he was beyond your control. Now he has a sudden rude awakening. He learns that you have a miraculously long arm with the power to hurt him (or at least scare him) even when he is some distance away.

In using the throw chain it doesn't make any difference whether you actually hit the dog with it or not. Even a near miss will have the desired effect. This is particularly true if the chain is first used when the dog is on cement or a similar hard surface, where it makes a noise on landing. It has a more immediate and lasting impression than if first used on grass. On grass you can miss the dog and, with his back turned as he goes away from you, he might not even know that you threw anything.

With the use of the throw chain I have found that the best results are obtained if the handler, immediately after throwing the chain, gets down on one knee and coaxes his dog in. When the dog returns praise him lavishly; assure him that as long as he stays at your side "that awful thing" won't happen again. In this manner, usually in a short time, the average dog will get the message — so long as he walks at your side he is safe. But if he should attempt to break away, that terrible thing will come flying through the air at him.

To those who have never used one before, it is amazing how effective a training aid the throw chain is. You should be careful, however, because too much use of a throw chain will often result in a cowed dog. You must use discretion. And *you must know your own dog.*

With Thunder, fortunately, heeling off leash proved no great problem. We were lucky.

After Fred had practiced heeling with Thunder on leash for about a week, using a lot of quick turns and sudden halts, the first time he unsnapped the leash it made no apparent difference in Thunder's performance. He still stuck to his young master's side as if glued there. Occasionally Thunder lagged a little on the about turns but Fred, by patting his leg and coaxing him in (plus the bait of a small piece of hot dog), soon cured Thunder of this flaw. Thus, within a few days Thunder was heeling off leash as well as when the leash was on. We never had to resort to having him drag the leash; nor did we have to use a throw chain. As I said, we were lucky.

Question: In the Novice class at an AKC obedience trial, when your dog is off leash, are you allowed to hold his collar and guide him to the proper position between exercises?

Answer: Yes. In the Novice class *only,* a dog may be guided gently by the collar between exercises or to be put in proper position for the next exercise. Open and Utility dogs are prohibited from being "physically controlled" at *any* time.

38

Thunder heeling free. (Note position of Fred's left hand, to prevent it from striking or distracting his dog.)

A perfect sit, rear view. (Notice the dog's attentiveness, awaiting the next command).

Step One: Walk out to the end of the leash, turn and face your dog.

Step Two: Call him, and reel your dog in to the front position.

The Recall

TRIAL REQUIREMENTS:
Upon the judge's order, "Leave your dog," the handler must give his dog the command and/or signal to stay in the sitting position while the handler walks to the other end of the ring. On the judge's order the handler calls or signals his dog to come. The dog must come straight in at a brisk pace and sit in a centered position in front of the handler, and close enough so that the handler could readily touch the dog's head without stretching forward. On the judge's order to "Finish," the dog must go smartly to the heel position and sit.

FAULTS:
A dog that does not come on the first command, moves away from the place where he was left, or that does not come close enough on the "Come" command, receives a zero for the exercise. Substantial deductions shall be made for slow response to the "Come" command, for the dog's standing or lying down, for extra commands to "Finish," and for failure to Sit or Finish. Minor deductions shall be made for poor or slow Sits or Finishes, for a dog that touches his handler on coming in or while finishing, or for a dog that sits between his handler's feet.

AFTER he had become fairly proficient at heeling, we began teaching Thunder the foundation for the Recall exercise.

The first step is to teach the dog to sit and stay. To achieve this, when the dog is in the sitting position swing your open right hand horizontally to a spot directly in front of his nose while repeating the command "Stay." Then move a foot or so away. If the dog starts to move quickly tap him on the nose with your open hand, jerking him back to his original position with the leash.

The "little gray rat" caught onto this exercise in about two training sessions. It wasn't long before Fred could walk out to the end of the leash, turn and face him, and Thunder would remain motionless.

Once this was accomplished the next step was to call, "Thunder, front" (or "Come"), while reeling in the leash until he was positioned directly in front of his handler. Fred then made his dog sit in the front position, pulling up on the leash while pushing down on his hindquarters.

In order to get Thunder coming in at a brisk pace, Fred gave him a tidbit every second or third time they practiced the Recall. He held the "goodie" in his closed fist, right in front. (In a trial the handler may not carry food, of course, and he must stand with his hands hanging naturally at his sides.) In this way Thunder soon developed the habit of coming in fast and straight. He never knew when there was going to be a choice morsel awaiting him.

From the "front" position Fred next ordered Thunder to "Heel," while simultaneously grasping the leash near the collar and taking a step backward with his left leg and guiding the dog around in an arc to the heel position, where he again made him sit. As with the conclusion of every exercise, Fred then heeled the pup forward one step, made him sit, and lavished him with praise.

I can't overemphasize the importance of praise. This is particularly true with a young dog.

Basically, dog training is merely a matter of combining firm correction when your dog errs with an abundance of praise when he performs an exercise correctly. These are two of the three principal requirements of successful obedience training. The other essential is daily practice!

As I repeatedly tell my training classes, you can't have a well-trained obedience dog simply by bringing him to dog school once a week. You *have* to do your homework! I insist that the members of my classes spend at least fifteen minutes a day working their dogs. If possible, of course, two or three fifteen minute sessions daily is even better. I don't believe the initial practice sessions should be any longer than fifteen minutes. Longer training periods are apt to result in a bored dog, and a listless, disinterested performance. To have an eager, attentive dog, brief but frequent training sessions are best.

After a week of using the leash to teach Thunder the foundation for the Recall, Fred began taking the leash off. And he began increasing the distance between himself and the dog. In a few days the young dog

42

Step Three: Make your dog sit in the front position.

Step Four: Guide your dog around to the heel position.

was doing respectable recalls from distances up to thirty feet. Further, with the ever-present hope for a tasty reward (he loved small slices of hot dog), Thunder continued coming in as fast as he could run — which was becoming faster daily as he grew in size.

In order to give his dog a relatively wide target for the Recall, in their early training sessions Fred stood with his feet spread about ten or twelve inches apart. And he made certain Thunder was centered before giving him his treat. Thunder's only problem was that his finishes were poor. He had a tendency to just swing halfway around — ending up sitting at an angle in front of his handler.

To improve Thunder's finishes on the Recall we did two things.

First, Fred closed his stance somewhat, to a position with his feet about four or five inches apart — the stance I prefer for trials. This made it easier for the pup to swing around to Fred's side.

Secondly, we went back to the method used initially in teaching Thunder the finish. When the dog was in the front position Fred snapped the leash on him and took a step back with his left leg, guiding him around in a wide arc to the proper heel position as he simultaneously brought his leg back to its original position.

This seemed to do the job.

After about a week of executing the finishes on leash Fred was able to remove the leash. Thunder's finishes were much improved. As with all pups, however, he had occasional lapses. Even several months later we found that the use of the leash every third or fourth time Thunder performed this exercise, helped to keep his finishes sharp.

Question: The scene is the Novice class. Thus far the big Irish Setter in the ring has done a very creditable job, having passed every exercise. He is now about to start the last individual exercise, the Recall. If the Irish passes this one, and if he gets through the Long Sit and Long Down, he has a qualifying score wrapped up.

On the judge's order to "Leave your dog," the handler puts her hand in front of the dog's face and simultaneously commands, "Stay!"

As his handler starts away, the Irish watches her for a few seconds, yawns, and lies down.

When the handler reaches the other end of the ring and turns around she is shocked to see her dog lying down. Fighting back a wave of tears (and the urge to kill), she sternly calls, "Shannon, Front!", whereupon the Irish (refreshed from his brief nap) rises and comes trotting nonchalantly in to the front position.

44

On the command to heel, Shannon swings smartly around to his handler's side and sits straight at the heel position, looking up at his mistress with big brown eyes that say, "Wasn't that great, Mom?"

Should Shannon receive a passing score?

Answer: With respect, first, to the simultaneous use of a hand signal together with the verbal command to "Stay," was this a double command? The answer is No; the Regulations permit the use of both a verbal command and a hand signal in this part of the exercise.

Now for the tougher part of the question. What about the dog's lying down after his handler gave him the stay command? Does this result in a failing score?

Again, the answer is NO. Under the AKC Regulations, a "substantial deduction" shall be made for a dog that stands or lies down, but the dog does *not* fail the exercise. Thus, while it is fairly clear Shannon won't be in the ribbons (unless the entire class goofs), he *will* earn a leg toward his Companion Dog title.

A trick you can use to obtain straight, and close, fronts — hold a tidbit between your legs.

"Stay!"

When your dog is steady, drop the leash and back up a few steps.

The Novice
Group Exercises

TRIAL REQUIREMENTS:
On the Long Sit, on order from the judge the handlers shall sit their dogs, if they aren't already sitting. On the Long Down the handlers will down their dogs upon the judge's order.

On the judge's order to "Leave your dogs," the handlers will give the command and/or signal to "Stay." They will then leave their dogs, go to the opposite side of the ring, and line up facing their dogs, for a period of one minute in the Long Sit and for three minutes in the Long Down.

FAULTS:
A dog fails the exercise if he moves a substantial distance from the place where he was left, or if he fails to remain in the sitting or down position, whichever is required, or if he repeatedly barks or whines.

A substantial (but not non-qualifying) deduction shall be made for a dog that moves even a minor distance or that barks or whines only once or twice. Either a substantial or minor deduction shall be made if the handler has to touch his dog or force him into the down position on the Long Down exercise, depending upon the circumstances of the situation.

O<small>NE MINUTE</small> can seem like an hour, three minutes an eternity.

There is nothing in obedience trial competition more nerve-wracking than the Novice Long Sit and Long Down exercises.

47

I much prefer the Open class; then at least you're out of sight. In Open you don't have to stand there motionless and watch in agony as your dog slowly sinks to a prone position during the Long Sit. Nor do you have to watch helplessly when your dog gets up on the Long Down, with only ten seconds to go. It is particularly heartbreaking, of course, when your dog had passed all of the individual exercises. You were already counting a leg toward your Companion Dog title, and perhaps even placing in the ribbons in your class.

Unfortunately it has happened to all of us who have done much showing in obedience. It's part of the game. Obedience training and competition wouldn't be any fun if our dogs were merely robots that we could wind up and have perform flawlessly. The elements of uncertainty and suspense make obedience competition the great sport that it is.

I recall a man I knew a number of years ago whose dog was always in contention for first place at the conclusion of the individual exercises, but the dog invariably broke on either the Long Sit or the Long Down.

As a cure, this man had the dog do a half hour Long Sit and a one hour Long Down every evening, while his master watched television or read the paper. It worked. After several weeks a one minute sit or three minute down was like pup's play to this dog.

The practice of making your dog do extended long sits and downs has considerable merit, although I feel a one hour down and half hour sit are too extreme.

In my Novice training classes we always double the required time in our practice sessions. Moreover, I have my students practice these exercises at home under the midday sun, as well as in the rain, to prepare them for any eventuality. You never know what kind of weather conditions you are going to encounter at an outdoor trial.

As a result, I am happy to say that whatever other exercises they may blow, it is very rare that any of my students' dogs fail the Long Sit or Long Down.

In teaching a dog the Long Sit the first step is to give him the "Stay" command while he is sitting at the heel position, with his leash on, exactly as you did when teaching him the Recall. If he starts to get up, or move, step in quickly, tap him under the muzzle, and sternly repeat the "Stay" order. If your dog is already doing the Recall this portion of the exercise shouldn't be any problem.

The next step is to walk out to the end of the leash and turn and face your dog. Then drop the leash and take two or three steps back. Again, if your dog moves, move in quickly and talk to him like a Dutch uncle.

Gradually increase the distance, day-by-day, until you are about twenty-five steps from the dog.

Eventually, go out about fifteen or twenty steps, and make your dog sit for two minutes (twice the required time).

Return around *right* side of dog. Don't let him move.

Stand at heel position until the order, "Exercise finished."

Thunder and his pal Barney, C.D.X. (owned by R.R. Richards) practice the Long Sit.

The down hand signal.

Initially, don't make your dog stay in the sitting position for more than fifteen or twenty seconds, but by the end of one week's practice he should be reliable for at least a full minute.

When you return to your dog walk around the right side of him back to the heel position. At the conclusion of the exercise don't forget the praise and/or tidbit.

The Long Down is taught in an identical manner. However, it is more difficult because you have to teach your dog a new command — "Down."

To put your dog in the down position grasp his collar with your left hand and pull his head toward the ground. Simultaneously give him the verbal command "Down," and also swing your right hand downward in front of his face, in a vertical motion.

At first, when you force your dog's head down to the ground his rear end may still be pointed skyward. Don't worry about it. He will get tired of this awkward position, so long as you continue to hold his head pinned to the ground. Eventually, he will lie down.

Once this is accomplished, repeat the procedure you used in teaching him the Long Sit. Back away a short distance, increasing the distance daily. If the dog starts to get up get back to him fast and really plant him in the down position, letting him know in no uncertain terms that you are *angry*.

In this exercise, as soon as possible omit grasping and pulling down on the dog's collar on the "Down" command. Train him to lie down on either, or both, the vocal command or hand signal. The reason for this is that in an AKC trial you *may not touch your dog* when putting him in the down position without losing valuable points.

If your dog should break and start to run away on either the Long Sit or the Long Down exercise, either restrict your early training to *on leash* sessions until you are satisfied that he is dependable, or use the good old reliable throw chain.

When you leave your dog on the Long Sit or the Long Down, or on the Recall, always step out with your right leg, the one furthest from your dog. This is in contrast to the exercises where you want your dog to move with you at heel. In the latter, start with your left leg, the one next to him. In this way your dog will quickly learn that when the leg next to him starts to move, he is supposed to move, too. On the contrary, when you move out with the opposite leg he knows that he is supposed to stay. This is a legitimate double command, and is used by many experienced obedience handlers.

Another legitimate double command I use on the Novice Long Sit and Long Down exercises is that as I stand facing my dog at the opposite side of the ring I fold my arms across my chest. This is in contrast to the clasping of my hands in a lower position (while holding a tasty tidbit) that I use in the initial stages of teaching the Recall exercise. Thus, usually in only a few sessions, your dog will learn that when you are standing with your arms folded across your chest it is not the Recall. He is to remain where he is.

Question: In a recent trial one of the dogs got up on the Long Sit and went over to pay his respects to a Miniature Schnauzer seated next to him. Before anyone had a chance to stop him the dog lifted his leg and proceeded to give the little Schnauzer an unwanted shower. Remarkably, the Schnauzer didn't budge from his spot.

When it came time for the Long Down, however, the bright little Schnauzer wasn't taking any chances. As soon as their handlers left the dogs the little fellow got up and proceeded to remove himself from the vicinity of his impolite neighbor.

Must the Schnauzer be failed?

Answer: An AKC representative was in attendance at the trial and after a short consultation with the judge he agreed this was an "unusual circumstance" of the type that merited a second chance. Consequently the Schnauzer was given another opportunity to perform the Long Down (positioned next to *another* dog), and he passed with flying colors.

Question: A friend of mine told me about a trial she attended where in the Novice Long Sit a Miniature Poodle performed the entire exercise in a "sitting up" position, with his paws waving in the air.

Should the dog be failed?

Answer: Penalized, yes (Chapter 2, Sec. 2 of the Regs.); Failed — No. To my way of thinking, a dog is sitting (as opposed to standing or lying down) if he is supported on his posterior. Thus, even when a dog is "sitting up" he is sitting, within the broad definition of the term. So long as the dog doesn't move away from the spot he should not be failed.

I had to chuckle at my friend's description of the irrepressible Poodle that pulled the stunt, incidentally, because I witnessed the same humorous sight at a trial one time. Again, it was a Miniature Poodle (there must be something about the breed). In that instance the judge did *not* fail the dog. At the conclusion of the exercise the little showman received a rousing ovation from the audience.

Use the collar to urge your dog to the down position.

If you have one of those rascals that doesn't want to stay down, step on his leash, as close as possible to his neck, to keep your dog down.

Fred and Thunder on way to the Novice degree. At top, at their first trial at Macon. Below, first again at Charleston.

Thunder's First Trial

THOUGH THUNDER was only eight months old, we decided to enter him in his first AKC obedience trial.

Ordinarily I wouldn't consider showing a dog in a trial until he is at least a year old, with a minimum of eight or nine months' training behind him. Moreover, I prefer to test a young dog in a few practice matches before entering him in a licensed AKC trial. That way you get an opportunity to see your dog's weak points; you have a chance to see where he needs more work. However, Fred was eager to find out what his "Thunder the Wonder" could do in competition. So, against my better judgment, we entered Thunder in the Novice B class in a trial in Macon, Georgia. I knew we would have stiff competition not only from the Macon and Atlanta dogs but from the northern Florida contingent as well.

As long as we were entering Thunder, I decided also to enter Clancy, our eleven year old Stanpoo, in the Open B and Utility classes. Clancy had earned his U.D. title five or six years earlier, and had not been in an obedience ring since. However, I figured that I would rather have something to do at the trial than just to sit around and worry about Fred and Thunder. Besides, I felt the exercise would be good for the old Poodle. To get him in shape I practiced daily with Clancy for several weeks prior to the trial. Nevertheless I wasn't expecting him to set the world on fire. In addition to being rusty, the old boy was having trouble clearing the 34 inches he was required to jump.

Early on a rainy Saturday morning we loaded our station wagon and set out on the three-hour drive to Macon. Thunder's class wasn't scheduled to start until the afternoon but Clancy had to be there at 9:00 A.M. for the Utility class.

Old Clancy seemed to enjoy getting back into action. In the Utility class he scored a respectable 192, earning 3rd place, and in a tough Open B class he scored 194½ for 2nd place, only ½ point behind the winner.

While I was pleased with Clancy's performance, my real concern was Fred and Thunder. Not only was it Thunder's first trial, but he had never before worked indoors. I expected that the noise and general chaos of an indoor trial, plus the new experience of working on rubber mats, might be too much for him. I had confidence that under the right conditions, and with a little indoor experience, Thunder would be capable of holding his own in any competition. However, the odds against him in this, his first trial, seemed just too great; I wouldn't have bet a Confederate nickel on Thunder's chance of winning.

The Novice B class started after lunch. There were some very good dogs in the class, including a great-looking Border Collie handled by a well-known Florida trainer, whom I recognized.

Thunder (number 52) was one of the last dogs to go into the ring. This was undoubtedly a good thing, as it gave him plenty of time to get accustomed to the bedlam inside the building. It also gave Fred an opportunity to study thoroughly the heeling pattern being used by the judge. By the time he entered the ring Fred was completely familiar with exactly where the judge gave each "Halt" order, as well as the "Fast," "Slow," and "About turn" commands.

When No. 52 was called into the ring I found a position well back from the ring and hidden behind some other spectators, so that Thunder wouldn't see me and possibly be distracted.

I couldn't fault Thunder too much on the Heel on Leash exercise. He worked as if he had been working on rubber matting all his life. Moreover, he moved fast and with his eyes glued on his young master.

If Thunder had any errors it was a tendency to forge ever so slightly on his sits, although perhaps I was being overly critical. In addition, I thought I detected a slight bump as Thunder rounded one of the posts in the "Figure 8." I knew that if this was true the judge would not miss it. She is an excellent judge, but notorious for her sharp eye and equally sharp pencil.

The Stand for Exam proved no problem.

I missed the Heel Free and Recall exercises because I spied a long-time friend and former competitor in the hall with whom I wished to talk. It had been a number of years since I had seen him. Besides, by this time I was satisfied that working indoors presented no problem to Thunder.

By the time I returned to the ring Thunder had completed the individual exercises, the dogs were on the Long Down. I asked Sally how

56

A two-headed poodle? No, just Clancy and a litter-mate practicing the Long Down.

Thunder had done in the other exercises. She replied that she thought he had done pretty well.

At the conclusion of the Long Down, and after she had an opportunity to tabulate the scores, the judge had all of the qualifying dogs return to the ring to award the placements. Thunder was one of those called. At least, he had passed.

"In fourth place," announced the judge, "is dog number 57. In third place, dog number 59," she continued, "and in second place the Border Collie, number 54."

At this point the tension among the exhibitors and spectators was mounting. This judge had a real flair for the dramatic.

"And the winner," she finally announced, "with a score of 196½ out of a possible 200, is — the young German Shepherd, dog number 52!"

The "gray rat" had taken first place in his very first obedience trial!

As they stepped forward to receive their award Thunder's tail was wagging from side to side as though to say, "What's so tough about this obedience trial bit?", and his youthful master was beaming from ear to ear.

The kids display some of the "hardware" collected in Novice wins.

Thunder Tries For
His "C.D."

SEVERAL WEEKS after his victory at Macon we entered Thunder in a trial in Charleston, South Carolina, sponsored by the Charleston Dog Training Club.

This trial was run by the club without the aid of a professional superintendent. I can say that I have never, anywhere, seen a better organized trial. Everything, from the rings, which were in a large armory, to the stewarding, and even to the delicious home-cooked, southern fried chicken lunches, was perfect.

The club had imported two of the premier obedience judges in the East. It had made every effort to make this one of the outstanding obedience trials in the Southeast. It was.

Thunder's class started after lunch. As luck would have it, he had drawn the tougher scorer of the two judges, Merrill Cohen. A witty and charming gentleman, Merrill has a well-earned reputation for being a fair but not overly-generous marker. After Thunder's 196½ at Macon, we, of course, had one eye on the *Dog World* award — which is given to a dog that qualifies in its first three trials with scores of 195 or better. Frankly, however, I was doubtful about Thunder's chances of scoring that high under this judge.

Watching from a strategic position at ringside, I had a perfect view of Thunder's work. For some reason Thunder had suddenly, that day, developed the habit of sitting crooked — not really bad sits, and not every time — but just crooked enough to cost him several valuable half points. Otherwise I didn't see much wrong with the pup's performance. He was alert; he moved fast. He worked with his head up and his tail going. He gave the clear impression of being a happy worker, devoted to his young master.

When it came time to award the placements Thunder, number 132, was one of those called. "The gray rat" had qualified again, and earned his second leg toward a Companion Dog title.

After awarding the fourth, third, and second places, Judge Cohen announced, "The winner, with a score of 195½, is the beautifully smooth-working team of the lad and his young German Shepherd, number 132!"

Thunder had done it again! *And* he had kept alive his hopes for a *Dog World* award.

As soon as Fred and Thunder had collected their trophies, including a magnificent silver clock awarded to the highest scoring junior handler, we piled into the car and headed back to Savannah. We had a long trip. And the next day, Sunday, we had an even longer drive — to the show where we had entered Thunder in his third trial; for us, a crucial trial because this time the pup would either win or lose a *Dog World* award.

Fred and I were up before dawn, determined to get to the trial on time. Clancy, our old Poodle, was also entered in this trial. His class (Utility) was scheduled to start at 9 A.M.

There was something strange about this trial that bothered me. Sponsored by the local kennel club, it was a combination breed show and obedience trial. There were over 1,000 dogs entered; yet Clancy was the *only* dog in the Utility class. Only he and one other dog were entered in Open B. In a show of this size, it made me wonder—but not for long. I quickly discovered why.

It was an outdoor show, and by noon the temperature would be in the 90's. The conformation dogs were under huge tents to shade them from the broiling sun. The obedience handlers and their dogs had absolutely nothing. The only shade in the obedience rings was under the judges' tables.

Arriving in the city well before 9 o'clock, we had difficulty locating the show site, which was a campground several miles outside of town. It was almost 9 o'clock before Fred and I found it.

Aftre paying to park the car in a distant cow pasture, I hiked about a quarter of a mile over to the Utility ring to report in.

The ring steward advised me that we were late. Clancy had been marked absent.

Frankly, I wasn't particularly upset. The only thing Clancy had not won was a Tracking title, for which I had never trained him. In addition to his U.D., he had done well in Retriever matches; he is an excellent gun dog. I'd brought the old guy along mostly for the ride.

While we were watching the Novice B class, one of the ringsiders informed us that we were in store for a treat. We were going to see, she said, "the best Novice dog in the country," a year and a half old Sheltie that had never been defeated and that was (like Thunder) shooting for a *Dog World* award that day.

I thought: 'This should be good — two top Novice dogs with identical records, meeting head to head!'

Thunder, number 55, entered the ring before the Sheltie. Despite the fierce heat, he performed excellently. From a vantage point adjacent the ring, I mentally scored Thunder at about 197½ or 198 in the individual exercises. I wasn't ashamed of him.

Then, at high noon, under that brain-searing sun, came the Long Sit and the Long Down exercises. In Thunder's group, all but three of the dogs broke on the Long Down. They got up and headed for some shade. Happily, Thunder (thanks to our frequent practice sessions on hot days) was not one of them. The pup stayed put.

The Sheltie, number 57, was in the second group, one of the last dogs to go into the ring. Having been alerted to her excellence, I closely studied her performance.

The little dog's heeling on leash was perfect. Like so many of her breed, the Sheltie was a sharp, quick-moving, precise worker. She was also perfect on the Stand for Exam. Her handler was obviously an experienced veteran. I was really impressed, ready to concede that this team was good.

Then misfortune struck.

On the Heel Free exercise, at one end of the ring the Sheltie left her handler's side and veered off to the left, heading for the shade beneath the judge's table. At the last moment, as if realizing her error, the little dog headed back to her mistress. But the damage had been done. In my opinion, based on experience as an AKC judge, the Sheltie had lost a *minimum* of two or three points.

It was a tough break. In that searing weather it might have happened to any dog.

Then came the Recall. The disaster was even worse. Coming in to her handler, the Sheltie suddenly headed again for the shade of the judge's table, swinging wide and this time pausing momentarily beneath the table before returning to her handler.

The AKC regulations state, ". . . the dog must come *straight* in." The Sheltie had not. Mentally, I deducted four or five more points, scoring her at about 192 or 193, at least four or five points lower than Thunder's score. In my opinion, the Sheltie had blown her chance for a *Dog World* award.

Apparently the judge saw it quite differently. After taking a long time adding up the scores, or maybe it only seemed a long time to me, she announced that dogs 55 and 57 — Thunder and the Sheltie — were to have a runoff (they had tied for first with scores of 195).

Then there was a snag in the proceedings. The Sheltie and her handler could not be found. Somebody reported that the handler was showing in a conformation ring. We'd just have to wait there in the blazing sun until her class was finished.

I glanced down at Thunder. He stood patiently beside his young master, head low, eyes half-closed, panting. The long, hot day had taken its toll. The pup was beginning to wilt. Fred didn't look so chipper either.

Being a native of Wisconsin, where the weather varies from subzero winters to sweltering summers, I know only too well how extremes of temperature can slow a dog and a handler. Since moving to Georgia I've learned even more about hot weather. It saps your energy, even your desire. Once you stop, it takes a real effort of will to get going again.

"You'd better keep your dog moving," I told Fred. "No telling how long you may have to wait. Walk him about. Just keep him alert, kill time, keep moving."

Fred nodded without enthusiasm. With Thunder at heel, he strolled back and forth next to the ring.

At long last Thunder's opponent arrived.

The judge announced: "The runoff will be the Heel Free exercise."

The two handlers and the dogs lined up.

"Forward."

Both dogs moved smartly ahead.

"Halt."

Both dogs sat perfectly.

"Forward . . . About turn . . . Halt."

Thunder's sit was straight. The Sheltie appeared to sit on an obvious angle. I let out a deep breath and thought: 'Well, that's it.' But I was wrong. For apparently the judge could not see the Sheltie's crooked sit. She continued the heeling pattern.

Finally, on the next about turn the tired little Sheltie was lagging so far behind that it could not be ignored.

At long last it was over. Thunder had won it.

If some of you have the feeling that this trial left a bit of a sour taste in my mouth, you may pass "GO" and collect $200. Fortunately, however, the conditions at most obedience trials are far better. And almost without exception the competence of obedience judges is excellent.

I would not like to see newcomers to obedience "turned off" by isolated incidents of poor facilities, or questionable judging. There is probably no cleaner, more honest sport in the world. If this were not true this writer would not have spent the past quarter century as an ardent obedience enthusiast. Nor would obedience trial competition be one of the fastest growing sports in America today.

Yes, there is room for improvement; there always is. But the sport of obedience can be proud of its achievements and progress since the concept of formal dog obedience competition was introduced in this country over fifty years ago.

But I digress.

After Fred had received his trophy we headed home. We were proud of the "gray rat." Thunder had not only earned his C.D. title, as well as the *Dog World* award, but he had gone undefeated in the process — at the ripe old age of nine months.

With Thunder, we had been lucky. He was not only blessed with keen intelligence, but he had the "eagerness to please" that is essential in a top notch obedience trial dog. Like the man said, "You can't make a silk purse out of a sow's ear."

Translation: The best trainer in the world can't make a trial winner out of a less-than-average dog. The best he can hope for is a dog that will pass, with fairly respectable scores. No, the "super dogs" are not only expertly trained, they have an inborn "something extra" — the flash and eagerness that separate the winners from the also-rans. This is something a dog either has or doesn't have.

It takes *both* — a lot of hard work *plus* a good dog — to produce a top trial dog.

Most of us in obedience are not breeders. We don't have 15 or 20 dogs on the premises from which to choose the best obedience trial prospect. Rather, we purchase a pup and, like the bonds of matrimony, he is ours "for better or for worse." Thus, we must try to make do with what Dame Fortune has given us. That's where the challenge comes in: trying to squeeze the best performance possible out of the material you have to work with.

Believe me, earning a 186 or 187 with an average dog is just as gratifying as scoring a 200 with a "super dog."

As I look back over many years of participation in the sport of obedience the most satisfying experience I've had concerned a different type of dog than Thunder. A real challenge.

In his first trial in the Novice class Gus wasn't too bad. He scored a whopping 110. He only ran out of the ring twice! In his next few trials he didn't do quite as well. But we were undaunted. We hung in there.

It wasn't that Gus was dumb. Far from it. The problem was that he couldn't see any sense in the regimented exercises and precision required in AKC obedience trials. He was a free spirit. Besides, on a sunny Sunday afternoon he thought he should be out chasing Brer Rabbit through the brier patches.

To make a long story (six years) short, Gus eventually earned his Utility Dog title. Moreover, he actually placed in the ribbons once or twice. (In those days the competition wasn't as tough as it is today).

The moral of this tale: Yes, it takes a dog with average intelligence to go all the way in obedience, but equally important, it takes *persistence* on the part of his trainer.

Question: Novice "A" judge Marshall owns and operates a training school and boarding kennel.

Mary K. has never trained her dog, Alfie, under Mr. Marshall, although a couple of years prior she had boarded the dog at his kennel several times. She had also taken another dog through his training class about three years earlier. She did not put a title on that dog. Can Mary K. show Alfie under judge Marshall?

Answer: Yes. The regulations only prohibit a person from showing a dog under a judge who has trained or boarded the dog "within *one year* prior to the trial."

Even if Mary were currently training *another* dog under Mr. Marshall she would still be eligible to show Alfie under him, since the rules say: ". . . if *the* dog has been trained . . . by the judge *he* may not be shown," etc.

Question: Now let's alter the facts a little. Assume Mary K.'s husband had previously put a C.D. title on a dog that he and his wife co-owned, although he had *not* trained that dog under Mr. Marshall. Under these circumstances, can Mary enter the Novice A class under judge Marshall?

Answer: No. Because the dog that had earned the title had been co-owned by Mary she is not eligible to compete in the Novice "A" class. She must enter Alfie in Novice "B".

Part 2

OPEN TRAINING

In the Fig. 8, use firm leash corrections to prevent lagging.

Practice stopping in various positions, so that your dog will be used to any Fig. 8 pattern that a judge might use in a trial.

66

The Open
Heel Free Exercise

TRIAL REQUIREMENTS:
The Heel Free in the Open class shall be executed in the same manner as in the Novice class, except that in the Open class the Figure 8 shall also be included in this exercise.

FAULTS:
Crooked sits; crowding or heeling wide; forging or lagging; failure of the dog or handler to change pace on the "Slow" or "Fast" orders; sniffing the posts in the Figure 8.

As I MENTIONED earlier, in my training classes I start the dogs heeling off leash after only four or five weeks of training. Thus, by the time they get into Open most are performing this exercise fairly well.

In obedience trials the only difference between the Heel Free exercise in the Open class and in the Novice class is that in Open the dogs are also required to perform the Figure 8 off leash. However, if a dog is doing the Figure 8 well on leash the transition is usually a simple one.

The most common fault in the Figure 8 off leash is that the dog may have a tendency to lag when rounding the posts. To cure this, do two things: Snap the leash on your dog and give him a sharp jerk every time he starts to lag. Simultaneously pat your left leg to coax him in, praising your dog when he is at the proper heel position. He will soon learn that every time he lags you are going to put his leash on him and he is going to be subjected to some firm corrections. If you persist, eventually your dog will be doing the Figure 8 off leash as well as when the leash is on.

The benefits of putting the leash back on your dog when he lags, or forges, also apply to his regular off leash heeling practice sessions. In addition, work him "double time," with a lot of quick turns, about turns, and halts. This will encourage him to keep his attention focused on you, as he will never know when you are suddenly going to change direction. In addition, it is particularly important when heeling your dog off leash that you don't forget the praise and/or tidbit. Make him *want* to stay right with you. Talk to him.

It is a good idea, of course, to start your practice sessions with some brisk on leash heeling.

Even after he had earned his C.D. title, Fred devoted the first two or three minutes of Thunder's daily training sessions to heeling on leash — thus keeping Thunder's heeling sharp. When you analyze it, even in the Open and Utility classes good heeling is *critical* if your dog is to place in the ribbons.

In the Heel Free exercise, although Open handlers are usually somewhat better than their counterparts in the Novice class, many still have a tendency to stop too abruptly on the "Halt" order, thus causing their dogs to forge. In addition, in the Figure 8 many handlers slow their pace too much, which will cost them valuable points. The object of the exercise, as with the "Slow" and "Fast" portions of the Heel Free exercise, is to determine how well the dog adjusts to the movements of his handler, not vice versa.

With respect to trial work, when preparing for a trial keep in mind that some judges will have you heel your dog almost up to the wall, or ring rope, and then have you halt. Normally your dog will expect an about turn at this point, and will start to make his turn before realizing that he is supposed to halt and sit. Consequently, in your daily training sessions occasionally practice walking your dog almost into a wall and then halt, making a firm correction if he starts to turn.

Another "trick" used by a few obedience judges, particularly if they have a large class and they wish to quickly weed out all but the very sharpest dogs, is to have you halt while performing the "Slow" portion of the heeling pattern. So also practice this during your training sessions.

68

If your dog lags off leash use a tidbit, and vocal encouragement, to coax him in.

Occasionally heel your dog right up to a fence, or wall, and have him halt and sit — so that he won't anticipate the about turn.

Unfortunately, in Open, as in the Novice class, an unnecessarily large percentage of the points lost are due to errors by the handlers, not their dogs. This is particularly true in Open A.

In the Open A class the handlers are non-professionals; the majority are working with their first obedience dogs. Not surprisingly, they not only continue to commit many of the same handler's errors they made in Novice, but they come up with some ingenious new ones. Moreover, despite the fact that they previously competed in at least three licensed trials in order to earn their Companion Dog titles, too many Open handlers are obviously unfamiliar with the AKC trial regulations. Knowing the regulations may mean the difference between your dog's passing or failing.

Question: Buck, a big, slow-moving young Rottweiler is lagging badly in the first part of the Heel Free pattern. Seeing this, his handler looks back and commands his lagging dog, "Buck, heel!"

Again, after an about turn, the handler looks over his shoulder and sternly commands his lagging dog, "Heel."

Should Buck receive a qualifying score, despite the double commands?

Answer: A dog that is lagging badly in the Heel Free may still qualify after receiving an extra command. However, by so doing, the handler will incur a deduction because the dog was lagging, and another *substantial* deduction because of the second command. A third "Heel" command would indicate that the dog is not under control. He is certainly not working with his handler as a team. This is a subjective decision for the judge, to determine if Buck should be failed for unqualified heeling based on the performance on the entire exercise. In all probability, however, Buck will lose more than 50% of the available points for the exercise — thus failing.

Drop on Recall

TRIAL REQUIREMENTS:
The orders for this exercise are the same as for the Novice Recall, except that the dog is required to drop when coming in on command or signal from his handler. And except that an additional order or signal to "Call your dog" is given by the judge after the drop. The judge may designate the point at which the handler is to give the command or signal to drop. The judge's signal or designated point must be clear to the handler but not obvious or distracting to the dog.

FAULTS:
The dog's prompt response to the command or signal to drop is a principal feature of the exercise. A dog that does not stop and drop *completely* on a *single* command or signal must be scored zero. Minor, or substantial, deductions shall be made for a slow drop, depending on the performance. All other deductions as listed under the Novice Recall shall also apply.

To MANY PEOPLE, the Drop on Recall appears to be one of the easiest of all Open exercises. They assume that since a dog has already been doing the straight Recall in Novice it is a simple matter to train him to drop on command. However, to teach a dog to perform the Drop on Recall *properly* is one of the most difficult tasks in all of dog training.

The trick is to get the dog to come in at a "brisk" pace *without* slowing up or anticipating the drop. Unfortunately, the smarter the dog, the more apt he is to anticipate the drop — particularly if considerable patience isn't used by the handler in his early training sessions in this exercise.

Too many inexperienced Open trainers will rush at their dogs, flailing their arms and screaming "Down," or they will throw a leash or a chain at them if the dogs don't immediately drop on command. Naturally, after a frightening experience like that, a dog is going to be hesitant about coming in the next time he is called. Put yourself in your dog's shoes, THINK LIKE A DOG; you'd be scared to come racing in, too, if you thought you were going to get a stern command, or, worse yet, have something thrown at you. The consequence, of course, is either a slow-moving, timid dog, or a dog that stops halfway in and automatically drops, or that stands and looks at his handler, waiting for the "down" command. Any of these faults results in a poor (if not failing) performance of the exercise.

To avoid such difficulties, when one of my students starts teaching his dog the Drop on Recall (which I *never* have him do, incidentally, until the dog has earned his C.D. title) I insist that he take it s-l-o-w and e-a-s-y.

The first time a handler has his dog drop I have him give the dog the verbal command "Down," in a pleasant, even casual, tone of voice, while simultaneously swinging his right arm vertically downward. If the dog does not drop, which is common, I have the handler walk toward the dog, but never in a threatening manner, and have him repeat the command in a friendly, pleasant tone. If the dog is still confused and does not drop, it is necessary physically to put him in the down position. However, this is done gently, with the handler talking to his dog reassuringly as he puts him down.

After the dog is in the down position I have the handler back away a dozen or so steps and then, with all the enthusiasm he can muster, call his dog to the front position. When the dog is sitting in front the handler lavishes him with praise, *and* rewards him with a favored tidbit.

Admittedly, using the method outlined above it will undoubtedly take longer to teach your dog to drop on command than if you employ harsher methods, including the use of the throw chain. However, you will have a fast-moving, happy-working dog if you will just have patience. With few exceptions, this is not an exercise that can be taught in a few days. It takes time, practice, and patience.

In your practice sessions, incidentally, have your dog do at least two or three straight Recalls for every Drop on Recall. This is added insurance against his anticipating the drop.

After your dog has become dependable on the Drop on Recall, and goes down immediately upon command, eliminate either the verbal command or the arm signal. You are not allowed to use both in an AKC

The "down" arm signal, a downward swinging motion with the right arm.

After your dog has dropped, call him in with great enthusiasm.

If your dog swings too wide on the finish, place a chair or other obstacle in a position where he has to finish correctly.

After using a chair, or other large obstacle, substitute a handkerchief. You will probably find the results are the same — a good finish. It will soon become habit.

trial. This is a double command which results in *failure* of the exercise.

With respect to the old question as to which is more effective, an arm signal or a verbal command, there are advantages to both.

The advantage of a voice command is that your dog will hear it and immediately respond (hopefully) even if he should be momentarily distracted and looking elsewhere at the time. For this reason I personally prefer this command. On the other hand, however, at obedience trials it seems that the public address announcer always chooses to make an announcement over the loudspeaker just as your dog is doing the Recall, and it is not unlikely that your dog will not hear your command. I have seen this happen many times — particularly at indoor shows — where the noise can be terrific. In the latter event an arm signal would be more effective — *if* your dog is watching you.

With Thunder, the Drop on Recall gave Fred considerable trouble. The Dutchman (at 75 pounds we could no longer call him the "little gray rat") had a stubborn streak as wide as the Rhine and he simply *refused* to go down on command. Thus Fred had to resort to a tactic I don't like to use unless it is absolutely necessary, as I mentioned above, the use of the throw chain.

It worked — sort of. Thunder quickly learned to drop on command as if shot. However, the rascal started anticipating the drop — and would come in at a pace that made a turtle look like an Olympic spring champion by comparison.

More than any other Open exercise, the Drop on Recall proved a real problem for Thunder. It was many months before he was performing the exercise well. Even when Thunder was entered in his first Open trial it was the Drop on Recall that worried us the most. It wasn't that he wouldn't drop; it was that he still occasionally anticipated the down command — or he came in at a snail's pace — which can be very costly, particularly when a half point or two can mean the difference between a dog's being in the ribbons or an "also ran."

Question: In the Drop on Recall, Duke, a frisky Boxer, dropped smartly in response to his handler's command. However, after remaining down for only a couple of seconds Duke rose to a sitting position, eager to dash forward to his master.

How should Duke be scored?

Answer: Unfortunately, Duke must be failed. The Regulations specifically state that a dog must *remain* down until called.

If your dog sits crooked put your foot out, just as he is sitting. This ensures that he *has* to sit straight.

Question: On the judge's order to "Call your dog," the handler waits for what seems an eternity (actually about five seconds) until his German Shepherd is looking at him, then commands, "Bruno, come!" When the eager, fast-moving Shepherd reaches the spot designated as the point to drop, the handler calls, "Bruno," and makes a downward swinging motion with his arm, the dog dropping instantly in response to the signal.

On the judge's order, "Call your dog," the handler calls his dog with a verbal command, whereupon the Shepherd comes in at a brisk pace and sits squarely in front of his master. On the command to heel, he literally jumps to the heel position, sitting straight at his handler's side.

How would you, as the judge, score Bruno's performance?

Answer: With respect, first, to the handler's delay in calling his dog after the judge's initial order, this will ordinarily result in only the loss of a few points. Losing a few points is always better than failing the exercise. The handler showed good sense in waiting until he was sure he had his dog's attention before calling him. One of the most common causes for failure of the Recall exercise is giving the "Come" command while the dog's attention is elsewhere. In such situations the dog either misses the command completely, or he is uncertain of it — in which event he will probably stay where he is, awaiting another command.

Despite the fact that the handler's delay in calling his dog cost only a few points, and despite the fact the dog faultlessly performed everything that was required of him, Bruno must nevertheless be failed!

When the handler called his dog's name and simultaneously gave him an arm signal to drop, he was guilty of an illegal double command. Under the Regulations, the dog's name may be used once immediately before any verbal command or before a verbal command and signal when the rules permit a command and/or signal. However, the name shall not be used with any signal not given simultaneously with a verbal command. Under the Regulations pertaining to the Drop on Recall exercise a dog must drop immediately on command *or* signal (not both). Thus the use of both the dog's name and a signal to "drop" is a double command which results in failure of the exercise.

Toss the dumbbell while your dog is excited.

Retrieve on The Flat

TRIAL REQUIREMENTS:
At the start of the exercise the dog should be sitting at the heel position. Following the judge's order to "Throw it," the handler shall give his dog a command and/or signal to stay, and then throw the dumbbell. The dog should retrieve the dumbbell and return with it to a position sitting directly in front of his handler. Upon the judge's order, "Take it," the handler shall take the dumbbell, and on the order, "Finish," the handler shall give his dog the command or signal to heel.

FAULTS:
The dog shall not move forward to retrieve nor deliver to hand until commanded. The retrieve shall be executed at a fast trot or gallop, without mouthing or playing with the dumbbell. On his return, the dog shall sit close enough so that the handler can readily take the dumbbell without having to stretch forward, but he shall not touch the handler nor sit between his feet.

IN MY OPINION, the most difficult exercise to learn in all of formal obedience training for a large number of dogs is the Retrieve. I would estimate that eighty percent of all dog owners who drop out of Obedience after they have begun Open training do so because of discouragement and frustration with the Retrieve. After spending many weeks, or even months, without any apparent progress they give up. It is an anomaly that a seeingly simple, natural act like retrieving is a far more difficult exercise to teach many dogs than anything else in their

Open training. For that matter, it is more difficult for many dogs than anything they have to learn in the Utility class.

This is an unfortunate situation because almost all dogs, even young pups, are natural retrievers; they love to retrieve *if* they think it's a *game.* Once they get into Open, however, where they learn that they *have* to retrieve the dumbbell, they balk. Suddenly it's no longer a game; it's no longer fun, and they refuse — with all the stubbornness of a Missouri mule!

Fortunately, there is a simple method of teaching the Retrieve that is successful with a majority of dogs. It is not successful with *all* dogs, but it works with most dogs. For lack of a better name I call it the "fun and games" method of teaching retrieving.

By no means is this method new, nor is it my idea; it is as old as obedience itself. Unfortunately, however, too many of today's Open instructors seem to have forgotten it and rely, instead, on the force training method. This is a mistake. With most dogs the Retrieve can be taught in much less time, and with less physical and mental anguish for both the handler and the dog, by employing the "fun and games" method.

Actually, the "fun and games" method couldn't be simpler. As its name implies, it is merely taking advantage of the dog's natural instinct to retrieve by keeping it fun, while patiently, and ever so slowly, incorporating the straight front and finish, etc., into the game. Before he even realizes it, the dog is performing the exercise.

One good way I have found to introduce a dog to the retrieve is to start by having him retrieve a ball, or one of his favorite toys, as part of the "play time" at the conclusion of his daily training sessions. This signals the end of formal training for the day. Ordinarily the dog will be full of vim and vinegar. Then, after introducing him to the dumbbell by teasing him with it, or having a tug of war, alternately throw the dumbbell and the ball for him during these "play" sessions. The dog will soon come to consider the dumbbell as one of his toys. Once this is accomplished you can phase out the ball.

For the first few weeks don't even concern yourself with straight sits or finishes. These should be introduced only after the dog is retrieving his dumbbell with gusto — and then, as I said, they should be introduced slowly and slyly — with *no* stern corrections. If your dog should suddenly decide that this isn't so much fun anymore, skip the sit and finish. Beat a hasty retreat. Go back to where you started, keeping it srictly play time for another week or two before again having him sit and deliver the dumbbell to hand.

By following the procedure outlined above, most dogs will be retrieving well in two months, or less. On the other hand, if you have to resort to force training it could take as long as nine or ten months before your dog is retrieving.

Another method of teaching the Retrieve, which I thoroughly recommend you try before resorting to the force training method, includes the following step-by-step procedure:

1. With your dog seated, place the dumbbell in his mouth. *Make* him hold it.
2. Repeat step #1 while you back to the end of the leash. Then step forward and take the dumbbell from your dog, praising him lavishly.
3. Repeat #2, but call your dog and draw him in to the front position before you take the dumbbell from him.
4. Repeat #3, backing away a step or two as you call him in. Gradually back farther and farther (dog still on leash).
5. With dog at heel, put dumbbell into his mouth. Command, "Heel" and walk forward. Walk only about ten yards, then reverse quickly, drawing dog to front position. Quickly take the dumbbell from him.
6. Gradually increase the distance you walk with your dog at heel. Always finish with reverse steps, drawing him to the front position (seated or standing, it makes no difference).
7. Seat your dog, put dumbbell into his mouth; drop leash and walk (or back) away about 15 feet. Call him. Gradually increase the distance, but keep the leash on. Stick to this until he brings the dumbbell from at least 50 feet away from you.
8. Gradually start making him reach a little to take the dumbbell, instead of shoving it into his mouth. Induce him to reach not only farther but *lower.*
9. Eventually place the dumbbell on the ground at your dog's feet. On command, he should pick it up. You quickly back a few steps.
10. Toss the dumbbell out a *few* feet; tell him to pick it up. Increase the distance little by little until you're really throwing it.
11. Start running away as your dog comes in, vocally encouraging him to speed up.

Sometimes in carrying out this program you'll have a stroke of luck. It depends greatly on the dog's temperament, and on the closeness of your relationship. But one day your effusive praise may so arouse his enthusiasm that you can grab the dumbbell out of his mouth and toss it and without thinking he'll go after it. That's when you quit for the day. For you've got it made! If it happens once, it will happen again. Then what was a tiresome job bubbles over into a game.

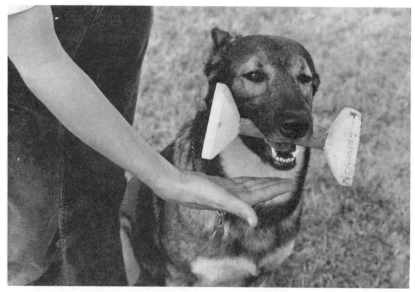

The "Carry the Dumbbell Method." Step One: "Hold it." (Tap him under the jaw if your dog drops the dumbbell, and give him a stern "No" command.)

Step Two: Tell your dog to "Hold" and "Stay." Back up to the end of the leash. After a few seconds return and take the dumbbell from him.

82

Step Three: Repeat Step Two but draw your dog in to the front position before taking the dumbbell.

Step Four: Repeat Step Three, backing away as you call your dog in. Pour on the praise.

With some dogs, however, this never happens. Then you have to resort to "force training."

With those lethargic dogs that can't be taught by the "fun and games" method, or the "carrying the dumbbell" method, the handler has no alternative but to use force training. To say that no dog should have to be force trained is nonsense. Regretfully, this is the only way some dogs can be taught to retrieve on command. I don't like to use this method. It does involve a degree of cruelty. In some instances, however, it *is* necessary if you wish your dog to continue with his advanced training.

In teaching retrieving by the force training method I throw the dumbbell out a few feet and guide the dog out to it by the collar. Then, when using a prong or so-called pinch-type collar, I twist the collar to apply pressure, forcing the dog's head downward toward the dumbbell. The application of more pressure at this point will cause the dog to open his mouth, to yelp in protest. At that instant manually insert the dumbbell in his open mouth while simultaneously releasing the pressure on his collar, *and* telling him what a good dog he is.

In lieu of a prong training collar, the same results can be obtained by twisting or pinching one of the dog's ears in order to make him open his mouth.

As I mentioned, using the force training method it may take many months to teach a dog to retrieve. I recommend it only as a last resort. I don't like to use it, and do so only when absolutely necessary.

Many dogs, in their early training, prefer to pick up the dumbbell by one of the bells (end pieces). The best method I know of for curing a dog of this habit is to pound nails into the bells, with the head ends of the nails protruding about three-quarters of an inch. This makes it impossible (or at least very uncomfortable) for the dog to grasp the dumbbell by one of the bells. He will soon learn to carry it by the dowel, as is proper.

With Thunder, Fred had introduced him to the dumbbell at about five months of age, strictly as a toy. As a result, retrieving was never a problem. The only difficulty with Thunder was that he loved his dumbbell so much that he liked to toss it in the air, or shake it from side to side, while returning with it. In order not to dampen Thunder's enthusiasm Fred merely gave him a mild "No" rebuke for these indiscretions. Eventually, as he matured, Thunder outgrew this habit, but fortunately he never lost his zest for the dumbbell.

In the early stages of his training Thunder also had the habit of mouthing the dumbbell as he sat in the front position. To cure him of this Fred rapped him on the top of the muzzle with one finger every

Step Five: Place dumbbell in his mouth and command your dog to "Heel." After a few steps reverse quickly and take the dumbbell from him.

Gradually start making your dog reach a little to take the dumbbell.

time Thunder would start to mouth or chew the dumbbell, while simultaneously telling him, "No." Thunder soon got the message.

Concerning the dumbbell itself, while the regulations do not permit any decoration on the dumbbell, the rules *do* allow you to paint the dumbbell. Take advantage of this by painting the bells of your dog's dumbbell a bright white. It will help him see the dumbbell, particularly at outdoor trials where the dumbbell might be partially hidden in the grass.

In addition to painting your dumbbell, always have two dumbbells, and practice with both. The reason for this is that someday your dumbbell may break when you throw it during the Retrieve exercise at a trial. Then the judge will give you a chance to throw another dumbbell, but if you have to borrow one from another exhibitor there is a chance your dog will refuse to pick up this new, strange-smelling dumbbell. He knows it's not his. So, I repeat, have at least two dumbbells which are used alternately in your practice sessions, and take both to trials.

Question: Upon the judge's order to "Throw your dumbbell," the small middle-aged woman swung her right hand, the hand in which she was holding the dumbbell, in front of her dog's face and told him, "Stay." She then proceeded to throw the dumbbell almost straight up in the air, the dumbbell landing about eight feet from her dog. The judge picked up the dumbbell and returned it to the handler, telling her she had failed the exercise.

The handler was dumbfounded. Was the judge correct?

Answer: No.

First, according to the official AKC interpretation of the rules there should be no penalty for a dumbbell having to be thrown again.

Second, while the Regulations specifically recite that the stay signal "may not be given with the hand that is holding the dumbbell," violation of this Reg. calls for a "substantial deduction" — not "failure."

Failure in this exercise should apply only for: A dog that fails to go out on the first command or signal; or goes to retrieve before the command or signal is given; fails to retrieve; or for a dog that does not return with the dumbbell sufficiently close so that its handler can easily take the dumbbell.

Place the dumbbell on the ground, on command, he should pick it up.

Toss the dumbbell a few feet; tell him to "fetch it." Increase the distance, little by little.

First, run your dog over low jump.

Calling dog over jump, on leash.

Retrieve over the High Jump

TRIAL REQUIREMENTS:
The principal features of this exercise are that the dog must go out over the high jump, pick up the dumbbell, and promptly return with it over the jump. The orders are, "Throw it," "Send your dog," "Take it," and "Finish." The height of the jump shall be as nearly as possible one and one-half times the height of the dog at the top of his shoulders (maximum 36 inches, minimum 8 inches), with the exception of certain specified breeds that, because of their build or size, are required to jump only once their own height.

FAULTS:
The minor or substantial penalties are the same as for the retrieve on the flat. In addition, a dog that climbs the jump or uses the top of the jump as an aid in going over must be scored zero. (Minor deduction for touching the jump). A dog that retrieves properly but goes over the jump in only one direction must be failed.

OLD CHINESE PROVERB say, "Never start jumping your dog until he is at least a year and a half old."

I say, "Old Chinese full of soy sauce!"

Seriously, the reason many professional trainers don't start jumping their dogs until they are physically mature is that they are afraid the dog may injure himself, perhaps permanently. There is logic to their

reasoning, of course, if you are talking about making a young, imma-
ture dog jump one and one-half times his own height at the shoulder, as
is required of most breeds in AKC trials. However, no one will ever
convince me that introducing a pup, as young as four or five months
old, to the high jump is going to do him any harm — so long as the jump
is kept low.

The principal advantage of starting a young dog jumping is that he
becomes so accustomed to the high jump that by the time he gets into
the Open class it is old hat — it presents no problem. Any animal authority will tell you also that an animal's jumping muscles must be developed — a gradual process. Hence, a young dog that is jumped mod-
erately develops physically for jumping. An older dog is handicapped
in this respect, if he has never jumped.

If you start your dog jumping at an early age, when he reaches physical maturity (it is unlikely he will be ready for Open competition before
that time) it is a simple matter gradually to raise the jump, inch by inch,
until he is clearing his required height. In addition, when starting them
early most dogs have an easier time learning *how* to jump. They quickly learn how to gather themselves for the spring, as well as how to
gauge the distance and height. On the other hand, I have found that it is
more difficult for many older dogs to learn these essentials. Moreover,
if they should hit the jump, and injure themselves, many older dogs are
extremely reluctant to try again. This is not usually as true of younger
dogs.

I recall very vividly an incident in point that occurred in an Open
class I was instructing a number of years ago. On the first night that I
introduced the dogs to a low jump a three year-old Great Dane
msjudged the distance and landed squarely on the top of the jump,
smashing it to kindling. The dog never did learn to jump; he developed
a mental block. He learned every other Open exercise, but he never
earned his C.D.X. — and he had been a *Dog World* award winner in the
Novice class.

I often wonder what that Dane could have done if his owner had begun his jumping lessons when the dog was a pup? My guess is that the
dog could have gone on and earned his C.D.X., and possibly a U.D. title.

I don't mean to imply that most dogs can't learn to be excellent
jumpers unless their jump training begins at an early age. Far from it.
My only point is that it is usually easier to teach a young dog. Moreover, in my opinion (which has been substantiated by a number of vets
with whom I have discussed the subject), it does the dog no physical
harm, so long as you use good judgment and keep the jump low.

In my training classes, as in most obedience courses, the first step in
teaching a dog to jump is to run him over a low jump (see photo at top

of page 88) while he is on leash. If the dog should balk, or use the top of the jump as an aid, a little upward jerk on the leash just as he is taking off will usually persuade him to clear the jump.

The next step, after the dog has gained confidence, is for the handler to give his dog the sit-stay command and step over the jump to the other side, with the dog still on leash. Then the handler enthusiastically calls his dog over the jump, again helping him with a firm upward jerk on the leash if the dog balks. When the dog is in the front position the handler should lavish him with praise and/or slip him a tidbit.

When the dog is performing consistently the handler can remove the leash. The dog should be leaping over the jump when called. Once this is accomplished, you can introduce the retrieve over the jump.

At first, position your dog very close to the jump (to reduce the temptation for him to run around the jump) and tease him with the dumbbell. While he is excited, toss the dumbbell a few feet over the *low* jump and *simultaneously* tell him to fetch it. If you have followed the steps outlined in the preceding chapter, and have a dog that loves his dumbbell, he will probably sail over the jump in quest of his dumbbell before he even realizes what he is doing.

Now comes the difficult part, getting your dog to return over the jump with the dumbbell.

Remember, as I stated above, when you throw the dumbbell toss it only a *few feet* over the jump. Again, the purpose is to cut down his angle and thereby reduce the probability of his going *around* the jump.

As soon as your dog picks up his dumbbell, move forward and pat the top of the jump with your hands, while enthusiastically calling him. As your dog starts to return you have to be quick on your feet. You have to back-pedal quickly so as to give him room to land as he returns over the jump.

If your dog returns over the jump with his dumbbell, really let him know what a *great* dog he is! You have the battle half-won. From that point on you can gradually increase the distance of your toss, and phase out the patting of the top of the jump on his return.

If you have one of those wise guys that persists in going around the jump, place one end of the jump against a fence, a garage wall, or some other obstacle to eliminate his running around that side. Then have your spouse, or someone else, stand at the opposite end of the jump, to prevent the dog from running around that side. Thus your dog has no alternative. If he wants his dumbbell he has to go *over* the jump.

After three or four days of practicing in this manner, taking the jump *both* ways should become second nature to your dog. Then you can eliminate the "barriers" at the sides of the jump. Your dog should be retrieving over the low jump consistently. Now start increasing the distance of your throw, and *gradually* begin raising the height of the jump. Don't rush it. There is plenty of time before you will have to start worrying about his jumping the full height required in trials. Unlike the Novice class, where you can have a fairly polished trial performer in four or five months (more or less, depending upon the individual dog and the dedication of his trainer), Open training takes most dogs considerably longer.

When your dog does reach the stage where you feel he is ready for Open competition raise the jump not only to the full height he will be required to jump, but set it about an inch or two higher, so that the regulation high jump will not look at all formidable to him in the ring.

Another tip for those of you who don't happen to be fortunate enough to belong to a club or training school having rubber mats, get yourself some rubber matting, and practice with it, before entering your dog in an indoor trial.

I have found that most carpet stores have odd sizes of "left over" pieces of rubber-backed stairway or hall carpeting that you can usually get quite cheaply. All you need is a piece about a yard wide and ten yards long, just enough so that your dog can get accustomed to taking off and landing on matting (turn it rubber side up) when retrieving over the high jump. Believe me, it is money well spent if you hope to do well in indoor trials.

Another piece of advice for those who don't particularly care to enter twenty or thirty trials before earning their C.D.X. title (I once knew a Boxer that took *fifty-four* trials to win his C.D.X.) is *learn to throw the dumbbell!*

A perfect throw is far enough over the jump so that the dog has ample distance to gather speed for his return leap, yet the dumbbell should be close enough to the jump so that the dog will immediately see it when he clears the high jump on his way out. In addition, the throw should be straight. If you throw the dumbbell off at an angle it not only makes it more difficult for your dog to find it, but it increases the likelihood of his returning *around* the jump.

Still another tip for those about to embark upon the voyage into Open-land: Take your jumps with you to the trials! I know, you are not allowed to drill your dog on the trial grounds. However, there is nothing in the Regulations preventing you from practicing down the block, or some other location removed from the trial grounds.

After you have driven many hours to get to a trial, as is frequently the situation, your dog should have a complete warm up, including the jumps, before going into the ring.

Coaxing dog over jump, off leash.

"Barriers" on each side will help deter your dog from running *around* the jump.

Question: The scene is the Open A ring, the exercise the Retrieve Over the High Jump. The happy-working Golden in the ring has turned in an almost faultless performance thus far. As he eagerly eyes the dumbbell, and fidgets anxiously in place, it is obvious this dog *loves* to retrieve.

After the handler has thrown the dumbbell, the judge pauses a few seconds and then orders, "Send your dog." Immediately upon hearing the judge's order, without waiting for a command from his handler, the exuberant Golden sails over the jump to retrieve his dumbbell. The handler, thinking quickly, calls after his dog, "Sam, fetch it!"

The dog makes a perfect retrieve over the jump, his tail going from side to side as though to say, "Man, that's fun!" His front and finish couldn't be better.

How should Sam be scored?

Answer: Unfortunately, the Regulations do not provide "extra credit" for an over-abundance of enthusiasm. Under the rules Sam fails the exercise because he left to retrieve *before* his handler gave him a command or signal.

Question: Upon the judge's order, the handler throws his dumbbell. On command from his handler the dog clears the jump, picks up his dumbbell, and returns over the jump to the front position, whereupon he drops the dumbbell at his handler's feet.

How would you, as the judge, score this performance? Should the dog be failed?

Answer: According to the Regulations, "Depending upon the specific circumstances in each case, minor or substantial deductions shall be made for . . . dropping the dumbbell . . ." In other words, the dog must be penalized but the number of points deducted is up to the judge. Most judges would deduct somewhere between five and ten points for this infraction.

If your dog uses the top of the jump as an aid, balance the top board so that it will fall, and frighten him, if he touches the top of the jump.

Success: Thunder retrieves over high jump.

95

Start with only two or three boards, placed fairly close together. Run dog over.

Step One: the "full draw".

The Broad Jump

TRIAL REQUIREMENTS:

The handler must stand with his dog sitting at the heel position in front of and at least 8 feet from the jump. On the judge's order, "Leave your dog," the handler will give his dog the command and/or signal to stay, and go to a position facing the right side of the jump, within the range of the lowest edge of the first hurdle and the highest edge of the last hurdle, and with his toes about 2 feet from the jump. On the judge's order, "Send your dog," the handler shall give the command or signal to jump. The dog must clear the entire jump and return to a sitting position immediately in front of his handler. The handler must change his position by executing a right angle-turn while the dog is in mid-air.

On the order of the judge to "Finish," the handler will give the command or signal to heel, whereupon the dog must finish as in the Recall exercise.

The length the broad jump is spaced should cover a distance equal to twice the number of inches of the high jump.

FAULTS:

Any dog that fails to stay until ordered to jump, that refuses to jump on the first command, or that fails to clear the full distance with its forelegs must be scored zero. Minor penalties must be made for failure of the dog to return smartly, to sit straight in the front position, or to finish correctly.

WE INTRODUCED Thunder to the broad jump when he was about five months of age.

Using only two boards, spaced about four or five inches apart, Fred at first ran Thunder over the jump on leash, using an upward tug on the leash just as Thunder was taking off, together with the verbal command, "Over."

Once Thunder was familiar with the broad jump, Fred began using three boards, still running him over. So far, so good.

Then Fred started what is frequently called the "full draw." Giving his dog the sit-stay command, with the dog seated a few feet from the boards, Fred stepped over the boards to the opposite side and ordered, "Thunder, over," while simultaneously reeling in the leash.

Thunder, like many dogs, decided to "tiptoe-through-the-tulips" — that is, he gingerly walked *between* the boards, without touching a single one. On his second try he was even worse, he walked right on the tops of the boards. His third and fourth attempts were no better.

We were not discouraged. Most dogs go through the identical procedure when learning the Broad Jump exercise.

To prevent Thunder from stepping on the boards we turned them on edge, so that the stubborn rascal couldn't walk on them. But Thunder the Wonder was one step ahead of us, as usual. He went back to his "tiptoe-through-the-tulips" routine, neatly stepping *between* the upturned boards. Thunder obviously had about as much interest in learning the Broad Jump exercise as I have in learning to become a belly dancer.

We were still undaunted. It was back to the good ol' reliable tidbits.

Fred tantalized Thunder with a piece of hot dog. Then he enthusiastically called his dog, still using the leash to encourage him to jump. In his eagerness to get that choice morsel, Thunder decided it was faster to jump the boards than to walk over them or to step between them. Hooray for our side!

After about three or four days Thunder was sailing over all four boards in quest of a "goodie." And he was doing it off leash.

Next, Fred started turning and back-pedaling, while Thunder was in the air, to a position alongside the jump (spaced about 2 feet from the ends of the boards). He made Thunder front and finish before giving him his reward. The first few times Thunder was reluctant to squeeze through the relatively small space between Fred and the jump on the finish. Fred had to guide him by the collar. In a short time, however, Thunder was finishing smartly.

Then it was time for the "semi-draw."

Rather than standing directly on the opposite side of the jump, facing his dog as he had been doing previously, Fred moved a couple of steps to the side. He then leaned forward and extended his arm (see photo Step # 2), to give the impression he was still in line with his dog.

Step Two: the "semi-draw".

"Look Ma, no hands!"

A well placed toe or knee will deter a dog from "cutting the corner" on the broad jump.

A low-set Utility bar jump, spanning the broad jump, will force your dog to jump — rather than walking between the boards.

It worked. Thunder continued to clear the boards and come in to the front position as Fred back-pedaled to a position adjacent the jump.

Gradually, day by day, Fred moved further to the side, as well as closer to the jump, although he continued to lean forward and extend his arm when calling his dog. After about two weeks Fred was able to stand right alongside of the jump and send his dog. Within another week he was able to do so without extending his arm, or leaning over. Thunder had learned the foundation for the Broad Jump exercise.

Fred then began to increase the space between the boards (again, very gradually) until Thunder was leaping a substantial distance. For the time being that was all we wanted. We didn't spread the boards to the full distance Thunder would be required to jump in trials for many months, until he was almost fully physically mature, until he was just about ready for Open competition. By that time performing the Broad Jump exercise properly was so deeply instilled in him that it presented no problem.

A month or so prior to Thunder's first Open trial we extended the broad jump several inches further than he was required to jump, so that the regulation distance would be easy for him in a trial. Thunder cleared it with ease.

One problem did arise, however, while Thunder was learning the Broad Jump exercise. In his eagerness to get to his tidbit Thunder began cutting the corner. He started jumping at an angle. To cure him of this, on one of his practice jumps Fred stepped in and "accidentally-on-purpose" gave Thunder a toe in the ribs, while the dog was in mid-air. Fred had to do it only once; Thunder never forgot that lesson. From then on he jumped right down the center.

Getting back to the "tiptoe-through-the-tulips" routine, this is probably the most common trick used by Open dogs when introduced to the broad jump. However, there are two things you can do to prevent this, or to at least make it more difficult for these connivers to walk between the boards.

First, try setting one of the boards on edge on top of the other boards, extending diagonally across the jump. This makes it more difficult for the dog to step through, or walk on, the boards. Frequently it works. However, occasionally you will find a rascal that still manages to step on or between the boards, stepping neatly over the upturned diagonal board. If you have one of these crafty knaves there is another trick you can use.

I would like to be able to take credit for the following idea. Unfortunately I can't. I don't recall where I first read or heard about it, but it's ingenious — and it works!

Left, turning the boards on edge will discourage a dog from trying to walk on the tops of the boards. Right, placing one board on edge, diagonally spanning the broad jump, will usually stop a dog from his "tiptoe-through-the-tulips" routine.

Obtain a Utility bar jump and set the upright standards on opposite sides of the broad jump. Then position the bar approximately ten or twelve inches above the boards, more or less, depending upon the size of your dog. The result — a jump your dog *can't* walk over! He has to jump, if he is to get over the bar.

You'll find that after several days of practice you can remove the bar, still leaving the upright standards adjacent the jump for a few more days. Your dog will probably be sailing over the broad jump. Then you can withdraw the bar jump standards. The results should still be the same.

If your dog should revert to his old habit of walking through, or on, the boards (which is not altogether unlikely), set the bar jump up again, straddling the broad jump. Even the most mule-headed dog will soon get the message.

This leads me to another point which I mentioned briefly before: One of the reasons dog training is so much fun is that for every problem there *is* a solution, assuming your dog is of average intelligence. The trick is to be smarter than your dog, which for some of us isn't always easy.

If one training method isn't successful with your dog, try another. Eventually, if you have patience and persist, you will come up with a method or gimmick (think up your own if necessary) that *will* work with your dog! This is where the fun comes in — trying to be smarter than your dog. Believe me, once you find the solution, and succeed in teaching your dog an exercise that you had thought hopeless, the self-satisfaction you'll feel will make it all worthwhile.

Question: The scene is the Open A ring. The bouncy little Bedlington (that's right, a Bedlington!) had not lost a single point up until the last individual exercise, the Broad Jump.

On the judge's order to "Send your dog," the flashy little performer sailed over the jump with ease and turned in a wide circle. While her dog was in the air, the handler turned at an oblique angle to the jump so that as the dog came in she was facing directly toward him. The dog sat perfectly in the front position. On his handler's command to "Heel," the dog swung smartly around to a flawless finish.

The handler sensed that she had a perfect score going. Immediately upon the judge's order, "Exercise finished," she joyously started tussling with her dog, praising him lavishly.

Obviously pleased with himself, the Bedlington began bouncing around the ring. When his handler told him to "Heel," and started toward the gate, the little ham dashed back to the judge, jumped up on him, and gave the surprised gentleman a big kiss!

Did the Bedlington earn that coveted 200 score?

Answer: The answer, of course, is "No." As a matter of fact he probably didn't score any better than 193 or 194.

Under the AKC regulations, in the Broad Jump exercise the handler is not allowed to turn at an angle to the jump (or, more accurately, he must turn at a 90 degree angle). The handler must turn so that he is facing directly toward the front. Thus, the Bedlington's mistress was guilty of a handler's error that cost her dog at *least* 3 or 4 points.

In addition, the rules state that in the Open and Utility classes a penalty *must* be imposed for a dog that does not respond promptly to his handler's orders *even between* exercises. Consequently, when the affectionate Bedlington ignored his handler's command to "Heel," and instead rewarded the judge with an unsolicited smooch, it cost him at least another 2 or 3 points.

Question: It's the Novice B class. Two of the dogs are obviously outstanding workers. Barney, a big young Rottweiler, is clearly enjoying himself as he heels, Figure 8's and Stands for Exam. Tail wagging, he is so eager to please that a couple of times he brushes his handler's leg on the turns. On the Recall, he comes at a dead run, skids to a slightly crooked halt but corrects himself and sits. His finish is an exuberant pivot, maybe half a degree from perfectly straight. He never takes his eyes off his handler or quits tailwagging.

The Rott's chief rival for the blue ribbon is Zerra, a Doberman bitch. Mechanically the Dobe is perfect. Her heeling is precise, her sits absolutely straight, her finishes correct. On the Recall she comes at a trot, head, ears and stub-tail down. On the exam she stands absolutely immobile, but her eyes warily watch the judge. Precise, correct, perfectly obedient, she goes through all the motions, but she shows no joy in her work at all.

If you were the judge, which dog would you score higher?

Answer: I know which dog I'd like to give the blue ribbon to — the Rott.

To me, there are few things in this world more pleasurable than watching an eager, fast-moving dog perform in an obedience ring — with his tail going, and his eyes riveted on his handler in *happy* anticipation of doing his bidding. It warms my heart; it renews my faith in obedience. Moreover, I know that without exception my fellow judges feel the same way. Further, the Great White Father at 51 Madison Avenue has always tried to encourage happy-working dogs.

The AKC regulations specifically state that, ". . . It is essential that the dog demonstrate willingness and enjoyment of its work. . . "

Obviously the Rott demonstrated "willingness and enjoyment of its work." Did the Dobe?

The Dobe came in on the Recall (at a trot) with her head, ears, and tail down. On the Stand for Exam, Zerra "warily watched the judge" during the examination. Is this a dog that demonstrates "willingness and enjoyment of its work," as specified by the regulations? Your answer is undoubtedly, "No." However, not so fast — how many points, if any, should be deducted from her performance?

On the Recall Zerra did come in at a "brisk pace," as required. The fact that she carries her head and tail low is probably an inherited characteristic. (I've had a few similar dogs, usually bitches). Moreover, a Doberman that does not keep a wary eye on a stranger is not a typical specimen of the breed, in my opinion. You can't "un-train" seventy-five years of breeding. Why should the handler, who had obviously spent many, many hours training this dog, and done an outstanding job, be penalized for something he had nothing to do with?

Thus, I feel, since the Rott did lose a couple of points for "crooked finish, brushing his handler," etc., the Dobe should be declared the winner.

The Open
Group Exercises

AS I MENTIONED previously, as an exhibitor I personally much prefer the Open Long Sit and Long Down exercises to the sit and down exercises in the Novice class. In the Open class at least you're out of sight. You don't have to stand there and watch in agony as your dog sinks to a prone position during the Long Sit, or gets up on the Long Down.

In Open the only heart-stopping experience you can suffer is when you return to the ring to find that your dog has moved, or laid down, thus failing the exercise. This is particularly disheartening if the dog had passed all of the individual exercises. However, at least you weren't there to watch helplessly as he blithely destroyed your dream of a leg toward his C.D.X. title, and perhaps a trophy.

Teaching a dog the Open Long Sit and Long Down exercises is usually relatively simple.

Your dog has already learned the Novice Sit and Down. The only difference is that in the Open class the Sit is for three minutes and the Down is for a duration of five minutes, in contrast to the one minute and three minute stays, respectively, required in Novice. Also, of course, in the Open class you are out of your dog's view.

If you followed my suggestion in the chapter covering the Novice Sit and Down exercises, and practiced having your dog perform these exercises for at least twice the length of time required in trials, the transition should be easy. The only troublesome part, and it is not usually too difficult, is getting your dog used to performing the exercises while you are out of sight, without his shifting position to watch for your return.

On the Long Sit, during your daily practice sessions have someone make noise, or cause a commotion, behind your dog — to prepare him for trials.

On the Long Down, have someone step over your dog, and try to distract him. The dog has to learn to be steady regardless of what goes on around him.

I recall an indoor trial a number of years ago where, during the Long Down, the ring wall behind the dogs was accidentally knocked down by some spectators. All but three of the fifteen dogs in the group immediately leaped to their feet. What did the judge do? Because three of the dogs did *not* break he *failed* the other twelve! As I mentioned, prepare your dog for *any* eventuality that might occur at a trial.

Speaking of preparing your dog for trial competition, at least two months before you plan on entering a trial begin giving your dog a daily practice trial. Get yourself a small notebook and list, one spaced beneath the other in sequence, the exercises required in the particular class. Date each page. Have someone judge your dog in these daily practice trials (or judge your dog yourself if no one else is available) and have him note his deductions under each exercise heading.

Frequent review of the notebook will show you where your dog is weak; it will enable you to concentrate more on that particular exercise, or exercises. In addition, your dog will become accustomed to having someone with a pencil and paper following behind him, as the judge does in a trial.

With Thunder, when we felt he was ready for Open competition, we began keeping a daily practice trial notebook several months before the trials in which we intended to enter him. It proved very enlightening. A review of the notebook after a few weeks showed that Thunder was far from ready. At least he wasn't ready to place in the ribbons. Thunder consistently took several steps forward before going down on the Drop on Recall. In addition, his "fronts" in both the Recall and Broad Jump exercises were poor. He had a tendency to sit in line with Fred's right leg, rather than centered between his feet.

By constantly studying his practice trial notebook, and working on the faults it pointed up, in a matter of just a few weeks we were able to improve Thunder's scores considerably.

When Thunder was consistently scoring 195 — or better — in his daily practice trials, we felt he was ready. It was time to try him in competition. So, for better or for worse, we began Thunder's Open campaign.

Question: It's the Open A class. At the commencement of the Long Down exercise, on the judge's order to "Down your dogs," one of the handlers put his finger in the loop in his dog's collar and gently pulled him down to a prone position. Is this permissible?

Answer: The regulations state that, "Depending upon the circumstances in each case, a substantial or minor deduction shall be made for touching the dog or for forcing it into the down position." (This is true not only in Open, but also in the Novice class). In my opinion, the handler in the situation described lost at *least* 8 or 9 points for his infraction. This may seem severe, but I feel a handler should definitely know better by the time he reaches the Open class. Ignorance of the regulations is gross negligence in the Novice class; in Open it is inexcusable.

Question: On the Long Sit, one of the dogs lies down as his handler is just in the process of going around him upon returning. Is this failure?

Answer: Yes, it results in a non-qualifying score. Under the regulations, the dog has to remain in the position in which he was left until the handler returns to the heel position. Thus the dog in question failed.

Question: In a trial some time ago, at the commencement of the Long Down exercise when the judge told the handlers to "Down your dogs," one dog went down almost in front of his handler's feet instead of at the side. Since the judge had not yet given the order to "Leave your dogs," the handler asked if he could down his dog again, to get him in a straighter position.

The judge gave a flat, "No," as his reply. He curtly advised the handler that his dog had failed the exercise.

The handler was shocked! Moreover, a number of experienced obedience people at ringside, including several veteran judges, were very surprised at the judge's action, to put it kindly.

I can find nothing in the regulations to justify the judge's arbitrary decision. In my opinion it was completely unwarranted. As one handler put it, "That kind of judge obedience doesn't need!"

Thunder Invades
the Open Class

W̲E DECIDED to begin Thunder's Open campaign by entering him in two trials on the same weekend, Macon and Atlanta. The first was the trial in Macon, Georgia. Both were combination dog shows and obedience trials, with large entries. At both shows it was the same old story — the obedience facilities were poor.

The Macon trial was indoors, in a large, beautiful coliseum. The breed rings were on the spacious main floor. However, the two obedience rings were cramped into a small, basement room beneath the bleachers, with no seating facilities, and with pillars in the middle of the rings. Frankly, I was a little surprised the obedience judges allowed the trial to be conducted under such conditions.

The rings were so small that in the Utility class the dogs didn't have enough room to advance far enough to give them a decent angle for the Directed Jumping exercise, with the result that most failed. The setup in the Open ring was just as bad, if not worse. The high jump was placed so close to the broad jump that after clearing the broad jump several dogs also jumped the high jump on their way back to their handlers.

About the only good thing I can say about the Macon trial was the caliber of the judges. Both were good, though tough. Fred's judge in Open A was Kent Delaney, from Chicago. I had competed against Kent as an exhibitor in the Midwest years before. He is an experienced and knowledgeable judge.

Unfortunately for Fred, Thunder (No. 12) was the second dog to go into the ring. This didn't give Fred much time to study the heeling pattern being used by the judge. To Thunder's advantage, however, he did not have to lie around for hours awaiting his turn (it was warm and humid in the building — or at least in the obedience dungeon.) When he entered the ring Thunder was still full of pep.

Thunder's heeling off leash was good except that he had a tendency to sit a little slowly. His Figure 8 looked perfect to me.

The next exercise, the Drop on Recall, was the one we were worried about. Thunder was not used to working indoors. I was afraid the noise of the crowd, plus the deafening public address system, might make him miss the "Down" command. This is exactly what happened to the Doberman that preceded Thunder in the ring. I was also afraid that instead of missing the down command, Thunder might anticipate the command, and drop before the judge gave his signal. This continued to be one of Thunder's weak points, despite the fact that for four or five days prior to the trial Fred had Thunder doing nothing but straight recalls, with no drop. And with a tasty tidbit as his reward for coming in at a fast pace.

Fortunately, my fears were not realized. Thunder performed the exercise almost flawlessly, with the exception of a slightly crooked front.

The Retrieve on the Flat and the Retrieve Over the High Jump proved no problem, although on the latter I thought I detected a slightly crooked finish. Nor did the Broad Jump present any problem for Thunder. Luckily, Thunder was not one of those dogs that thought he could gain extra credit by taking the adjacent high jump on his way back to his handler.

Considering the slightly slow sits and other minor errors, I scored the gray rat about 196 and wondered whether that would be good enough to hold up through the remainder of the class.

There was one dog in the class that caught my eye, a black Cocker Spaniel from Florida. The dog was quick-moving and precise. Her heeling and Figure 8 were almost perfect. If the dog lost any points it was because of a tendency to sit a little too close to her handler, touching her leg slightly.

On the Recall and Retrieve on the Flat I couldn't fault the Cocker.

Then came the High Jump. For the first time, the sharp little worker had an obvious deduction, a bad crooked front. In addition, on the finish the dog leaped up while going to the heel position and from where I was sitting it appeared she put her front paws on her mistress prior to swinging around to her side. But I wasn't sure.

On the Broad Jump the Cocker's front could have been a little straighter.

I scored the Cocker at about 196. After watching the remainder of the class I was convinced it was between Thunder and the Cocker for first place, perhaps a run-off.

110

After he had tabulated the scores Kent stood up and Fred and I were sure he was going to call for dogs number 12 and 48, Thunder and the Cocker, for a run-off. But no, he merely read off the numbers of the qualifying dogs and had them all come into the ring. There was to be no run-off, but which dog had won?

"In an obedience trial," Kent announced to the audience, " a perfect score is 200. Unfortunately," he said, "we didn't have anything close to that today, although we did have some very good working dogs."

My heart sank; what did he mean by "close" to 200? We were trying for at least a 195, to give Thunder a shot at his second *Dog World* Award.

After pausing a few seconds he continued, "In first place is . . . dog number 12, the German Shepherd, with a score of 196."

Fred beamed and Thunder smiled smugly (I swear it!) as they stepped forward to receive their trophy.

The Cocker, as we had thought, was not far behind. She scored a 195½ for 2nd place. In third place was a nice-working Giant Schnauzer, a breed not seen too frequently in obedience rings.

Immediately after the conclusion of Fred's class we were off to Atlanta, for the trial at nearby Stone Mountain the following day.

We were worried about the Atlanta trial. It was a huge combination dog show and obedience trial, with almost 3,000 dogs entered. We knew that in addition to most of the same dogs that competed in Macon, Thunder would be up against Atlanta's best. Atlanta is a hotbed of obedience enthusiasts.

Fortunately for us, Thunder's class didn't start until 2:00 in the afternoon, so, for a change, we didn't have to worry about getting up at the crack of dawn. It gave Sally and me a chance to sample Atlanta's famed "underground" night life. By the time we arrived back at our motel, Fred and Thunder had been asleep for hours in the adjacent room.

The next day we somehow managed to get out to Stone Mountain State Park about noon. We wanted to give Thunder plenty of opportunity to get used to the grounds, and the crowd, before going into the ring.

When I saw the obedience set-up I was disgusted.

The conformation rings were in a huge open-sided building, with a roof to protect exhibitors and dogs from sun and rain. The obedience rings were set up on a patch of dirt adjacent the building, with nothing to protect them from the elements. It had rained the night before. The surface on which the obedience dogs had to work was a quagmire. Another example of the second-class status afforded to obedience exhibitors — even though we pay the same entry fee as breed exhibitors.

On the brighter side, again the selection of judges had been excellent. Fred's judge was a delightfully charming and gracious woman, Mrs. Aldythe Comstock, under whom I had shown frequently when she was living in the Chicago area. She and her husband are now retired and living in Florida.

Before he went into the ring I told Fred, "Whatever score you and Thunder receive is exactly what you will have earned; you are showing under one of the best obedience judges in the country. Regardless of how you do, be a good sportsman."

Fred replied, "Don't worry Dad, I know that no dog is going to win every time — I've seen you and your dogs blow too many trials." (I didn't think that reminder was necessary; sometimes the little wise guy reminds me a lot of his mother.)

Again, as in the trial the day before, Thunder, number 12, was the second dog to go into the ring, which didn't give Fred much opportunity to study the heeling pattern.

From where I was standing (no seats), Thunder's heeling looked excellent. He was working with enthusiasm. However, I thought his drop on the Recall was a little slow, perhaps due to the sloppy surface. Moreover, in the Retrieve Over the High Jump his front appeared crooked, and on the Broad Jump I thought both his front and finish looked *slightly* crooked, although perhaps I was being overly critical. In any event, it was not a bad performance. I was satisfied. Now it would be up to the rest of the class to catch him.

The little Cocker from Florida didn't look as flashy or precise as she had the day before. She appeared tired, though she still managed to turn in a nice performance.

When it came time for the Long Sit and the Long Down I was a little worried about Thunder, particularly on the Long Down. He was not used to lying in mud. Fortunately he passed without difficulty. Some of the other dogs, however, didn't fare so well.

There was one handler in the second group that I felt especially sorry for. He had a young St. Bernard that was unquestionably one of the finest working Saints I have ever seen in an Open ring. Frankly, he was one of the dogs that I was worried about after watching his beautiful job in the individual exercises. I have never seen a Saint that could jump like that one. Unfortunately, the Saint sat up with *only ten seconds* to go on the five minute Long Down. As I learned later from his handler, it would have been the dog's first leg toward his C.D.X. title. In addition, in my opinion, he would have certainly been in the ribbons. To the handler's credit, he took it with good grace. With a smile

Thunder sailing over high jump at Atlanta.

and philosophical shrug he said, "Maybe next time," as he scratched the big Saint's head and told him what a good boy he was. Obedience could use more exhibitors like this one.

After Mrs. Comstock completed her paper work she called all of the qualifying dogs into the ring. Thunder was one of them.

I had not watched all of the dogs in the class work, so I had no idea where Thunder had placed, or if he had placed at all. It had been a large class, with a lot of good-working dogs.

The judge first awarded the fourth, third, and second place winners. Thunder was not one of them.

"And in first place," she announced, as a hush fell over the large crowd that had gather at ringside, "with a score of 196½ is . . . the German Shepherd, dog number 12!"

In addition to winning his class, Thunder was also second high in trial, highest scoring Shepherd, highest scoring dog from the Working Group, and Fred won a beautiful silver platter for highest scoring junior handler.

Next it was on to Jacksonville, Florida, where Thunder Over Dixie would try to earn his C.D.X. title. And we would be trying to keep intact his record of never having been beaten in competition. Plus which, Thunder would be shooting for his second *Dog World* Award.

"Old Clancy" (2nd dog from left) proves himself still a winner in Obedience at 11 years of age—six years after winning his "U.D." This winning quartet gives its own evidence of the diversity of breeds currently starring in Obedience.

Thunder Bombs!

THUNDER flunked the Jacksonville trial. Fred gave a disqualifying double command on the Broad Jump exercise. He raised his arm in an upward swinging movement while simultaneously giving his dog the verbal command, "Thunder, over!"

The kid immediately realized what he had done, but it was too late. When he came out of the ring he just stared at the ground in disbelief. He said, "Dad, I just wasn't thinking. I guess I was nervous — I knew it was the last exercise and I was too anxious to get it over with." Then he asked, "Are you mad?"

I said, "Fred, if I had a dollar for every point I've cost my dogs in the ring over the past 20 years I could retire. Forget it. Besides," I added, "Thunder's heeling today looked like he was plodding through a plowed field after a rainstorm." (Actually I thought Thunder's work had been pretty good — I scored him at about 196 or 197. First place in the class was 192.)

The boy was disgusted with himself and discouraged. I didn't want this. Fred had worked hard with his dog. Regardless of the fact that he had blown one trial, I was proud of him. He had done an excellent job of training. To err is human (you may quote me if you wish), and the fact that in six trials he had one brief mental lapse was nothing to be ashamed of. On the way home we stopped and bought him a steak dinner (with a large "doggy bag" for Thunder). Nevertheless, it was a long quiet ride home. Fred was a very disappointed youngster. Finally he broke a long silence. "At the next trial," he said, "we're going to get a 200." And he scratched the ears of the big gray dog asleep next to him on the back seat. Then I knew everything was O.K.

As for the trial itself, you won't believe this but I have absolutely nothing to complain about (I must be mellowing in my old age). Actually, it was a beautifully organized trial, efficiently run, with excellent ring facilities and good stewards. It was just what one would expect of a trial with which Blanche Carlquist was associated.

One thing in particular stands out in my mind, and always will, when I recall the Jacksonville trial. There was Blanche Carlquist, one of the foremost and respected obedience figures in America, and what was she doing? Between classes Blanche was out pushing a broom around the rings, to make certain they were immaculate. What more need be said about Blanche Carlquist, and the type of person she is?

And the judges—they couldn't have been better. Fred's judge was Barbra Goodman, the vivacious blond bombshell from Chicago. When Fred pulled his "goof" I don't think there was anyone in the place more shocked and disappointed than Barb. As Fred and Thunder were leaving the ring Barb turned to the audience and said, "Let's give them a big hand," and she joined the crowd in applauding the boy and his dog for their performance. This is the type of gesture which distinguishes a truly fine judge.

To get back to Fred's handling error, it emphasizes something I have always tried to instill in my students: once you enter the ring, there is little you can do about how your dog is going to perform that day. It's too late. Thus, all you can do is concentrate on being a good handler. Try not to lose any points for *your* mistakes. Let your dog's score reflect *his* performance.

I believe one of the most rewarding second-hand compliments I ever received occurred a few months ago when one of my students entered her first trial, in the Novice A class. Unfortunately the dog blew the Recall, but as my student was leaving the ring the judge stopped her and said, "I'm very sorry your dog failed, but I just wanted to tell you that you are one of the finest novice handlers it's ever been my privilege to judge." And he asked her where she trained.

She related the conversation to me when she came out of the ring. Then we both went over to her dog and wrung his neck.

"If At First..."

It was several months after the Jacksonville trial before Thunder got another opportunity to try for his Companion Dog Excellent title. Obedience trials in the Southeast are few and far between, unlike the Midwest and some other parts of the country where you can find a trial within driving distance almost every weekend.

Thunder's next trial was in Atlanta. Run by the Atlanta Obedience Club, this was not a combination breed show and obedience trial. It was strictly obedience, with the result that the facilities, organization, and running of the trial were far superior to the conditions usually encountered by obedience exhibitors at combination breed and obedience shows in this area. It was an excellent trial. Moreover, Thunder's judge was the internationally famous Beau Brummel from north of the border, the dapper Jake Giacomelli.

I had been looking forward to meeting Mr. Giacomelli for a long time and was fortunate to have an opportunity to chat with him following the judging.

Oh yes, Thunder. How did he do? I'd rather forget it.

It was an indoor trial, with not too much room — at least for Thunder. On the Retrieve On the Flat, when Fred threw the dumbbell it landed a little bit to the side of the center mat, so that when Thunder picked it up he was staring at the high jump. He debated whether to take the jump or to come straight in. He took about two steps forward and then froze, looking first at the jump and then at Fred, awaiting some sort of instruction.

Fred let him stand there for a short while, hoping Thunder would come straight in. No dice. Thunder stood there motionless, looking for all the world like a statue of a gray wolf (I wished I had my camera). Finally, after about seven or eight seconds, when it was obvious Thunder was hopelessly confused, Fred called him in to the front position.

There went Thunder's C.D.X., at least for the time being. He would have to wait another three weeks for the next trial, at Charleston, S.C.

The Charleston trial, as always, was excellently organized and run. In my opinion, the Jacksonville and Charleston trials are two of the premier obedience trials in the Southeast. In addition to good judges, and excellent ring facilities in a completely air-conditioned building, the hospitality of the Charleston trial committee was great.

Unfortunately, Saturday night, the night before the trial, we had a minor catastrophe. Fred came down sick. The flu. Not serious, but he was in no condition to make the trip to Charleston the next day. Thunder was entered in Open A, thus I could not handle him in the ring, since obedience judges are not allowed to show in the "A" classes. We had no alternative — Sally would have to show Thunder.

Many eons ago, when we were first married, Sal had trained a dog through Novice, but she had never set foot in an Open ring, and she had never worked with Thunder.

Sunday morning I got Sal up a little earlier than she would have liked. "Move it, Lard," I said, in my own endearing manner, "You've got to practice."

She buried her head under the pillow, muttering that she thought it had just been a bad dream. "No," I assured her, "this is your day of glory."

After spending about a half hour attempting to pick out a suitable costume (I tried unsuccessfully to explain to her that this was a dog trial, not a fashion show), she finally selected a blue and white plaid pants suit. Stunning. Now that that critical decision was made, there were only 15 minutes left before we had to take off for Charleston.

I ushered Sal out to the back yard and proceeded to put her and Thunder through a simulated Open trial, sans the Long Sit and Long Down, which we didn't have time for.

Surprisingly, Thunder worked pretty well. And Sal didn't look too bad as a handler. My gloom diminished slightly, though I was not exactly brimming with confidence as we loaded the car and headed for Charleston.

Arriving in Charleston well before Thunder's class was scheduled to begin, Sal asked me if she should go down the block and do a little practicing? "Forget it," I grumbled, "you'd be better off finding a church. Besides," I added, "let's watch the Novice class, some of my students are competing."

In the Novice B class, Misty, a Collie from my school, performed nicely, in my opinion. Not first place, but in the ribbons. At the conclusion of the Long Sit and Long Down, while the judge was tabulating the scores, I told Misty's handler to take her dog outside and wake her up, she might be in a run-off.

No sooner had Misty and her handler returned to the building when the judge called her into the ring. It was to be a run-off between the Collie and a Sheltie, for 3rd place (with very creditable scores of 195).

The run-off didn't take long. The Sheltie had been asleep next to his master until the run-off was announced. The Collie was wide awake and sharp, thanks to her little trip outdoors. Misty won it, thus not only capturing third place in the class, but finishing her C.D.

I was pleased, naturally, but I am never completely happy with a third place, particularly with a good-working dog like Misty that I felt had Highest in Trial potential.

In Novice A we fared better. Charley, a precocious Pekingese from my school, took first, with a score of 197.

Then it was time for Thunder's class. Thunder, Number 42, was the second dog to go into the ring. This didn't give Sal much time to study the heeling pattern.

Frankly, I was pleasantly surprised with Thunder's performance, as well as with Sally's handling. The only things I could fault them for was a tendency on the part of Thunder to come in a little slowly on the Recall and Retrieve exercises. Otherwise I couldn't find too much wrong. I didn't see how the judge could score him any less than 196 or 196½. I thought Thunder had second place, or at least third, sewed up.

After the judge had added the scores he called the qualifying dogs into the ring. Number 42 was one of them. Even if he hadn't placed, Thunder had at least qualified, thus earning his 3rd leg and his C.D.X. title.

"In fourth place," announced the judge, "is dog number 41, in third dog number 45, and in second, with a score of 196½ is the Irish Setter, No. 49."

"Nuts," I thought, "Thunder didn't place."

"And in first place," continued the judge, "with a score of 197, is the smooth-working team of the Shepherd No. 42 and his handler." Sally beamed as she and Thunder stepped forward (I thought she was going to kiss the judge), and my mouth fell open in disbelief. Thunder had not only won his class, but he had tied for Highest Scoring Dog in Trial — working with a handler that he had practiced with for all of fifteen minutes.

Then came the run-off for H.I.T., between Thunder and Charley, the Pekingese. Having been Charley's instructor for a year I knew him

"High in Trial! I don't believe it."

well; I knew his faults and his strong points. His forte was heeling. He was super-quick, and precise.

The run-off, announced the judge, was to be off-leash heeling. Both handlers, and their dogs, entered the ring and lined up.

"Forward," ordered the judge. "Halt." Both dogs sat perfectly. "Forward, about turn, halt." Charley's sit was a fraction from perfect. The judge pointed to Sally and Thunder. It was over, Thunder had won it. His first H.I.T.

By the time the trophy committee had completed its task of figuring out the special awards winners it was apparent that Savannah had done well. In addition to 1st and 2nd highest scoring dogs in the trial, first place in Novice A, first in Open A, and first in Versatility (Thunder), our dogs had won: highest scoring Collie, highest scoring German Shepherd, highest scoring dog from the Working Group, highest scoring dog from the Toy Group, and highest scoring Terrier.

I was afraid that the Charleston Dog Training Club wouldn't send us any entry forms for its next trial.

120

Part 3

UTILITY TRAINING

"Thunder, heel!" (A sweeping motion of the left hand).

"S-t-a-n-d."

"Down!"

Signal Exercise

TRIAL REQUIREMENTS:

The heeling is done in the same manner as in the Heel Free exercise except that the handler uses signals only. The handler may signal his dog to walk at heel and then, on specific order from the judge, the handler and dog execute a left turn, right turn, about turn, halts, slow, normal and fast.

On order from the judge, the handler signals his dog to stand in the heel position. The handler then signals his dog to "Stay," upon the judge's order to "Leave your dog," and goes to the far end of the ring. On separate signals from the judge the handler will signal his dog to Drop, to Sit, to Come, and to Finish.

The principal features of this exercise are the heeling of the dog, the "Come" on signal, and the prompt response to the other signals.

FAULTS:

A dog that fails, on a single signal from the handler, to stand or remain standing where left, or to drop, or to sit and stay, or to come, or that receives a command or audible signal from the handler to do these parts of the exercise shall be scored zero. All of the deductions listed under the Heel and Recall exercises shall also apply to this exercise.

THE SIGNAL EXERCISE is the easiest of the Utility exercises to teach most dogs. However, there are two areas of the exercises that prove a little difficult for many dogs, and which frequently require considerable practice before a dog is performing the exercise properly.

First, many dogs initially insist upon taking two or three steps forward after their handlers have given them the signal to halt and stand. The best cure for this is a good stern "No" command if the dog doesn't halt immediately. In addition, in his early training it is frequently helpful to step in front of your dog as you give him the stand signal. Thus he cannot continue forward, since your leg is blocking his way. He *must* halt immediately. He will soon get the idea.

The other, and more serious, problem with many would-be Utility dogs is the dog's failure to keep his attention directed toward his handler after the handler has left him in the standing position and gone to the opposite end of the ring. With this type of dog, who is "counting the house" rather than watching his handler, the dog is apt to miss the "Down" or "Sit" signals, or both. The best remedy I know for curing this type of dog is to throw a leash at him if you don't have his attention during your practice sessions. As I have mentioned before, most dogs *hate* to have a leash (or throw chain, or chain collar) thrown at them. The result is that your dog will watch you when you go to the opposite end of the ring, if for no other reason than to see if you are going to throw that "terrible thing" at him.

Once you have your dog's undivided attention you have the battle half-won.

With respect to the best hand, or arm, signals to use for several commands, there is some difference of opinion among experienced dog trainers. The signals I prefer are as follows:

For the "heel" signal I pass my left hand directly in front of the dog's face, while simultaneously stepping forward with my left leg. In his early training it is advisable, of course, to also give your dog a simultaneous verbal command to "Heel." In a short time, however, he should be responding to the hand signal alone.

For the "Stand" signal I use a forward horizontal sweeping motion alongside of and forward of the dog's head with my *right* hand. This is a very similar motion to the arm motion used initially in teaching your dog to stand (while simultaneously pulling him forward with the leash.) Many other trainers merely pass their left hand in front of their dog's face to signal the halt-stay. I wouldn't recommend this "casual" signal until your dog is completely reliable on the stand-stay. Either signal is permissible, however, under the Regulations.

As for the "Down" signal, almost all seasoned handlers use a downward swinging movement with the right arm. The reason I prefer this signal is because it is similar to the arm movement used when throwing

124

"Sit!"

"Come!"

125

a leash at the dog — which is sometimes necessary in the early stages of teaching him to go down.

The "Sit" signal I use is an upward swinging motion of the *left* arm. The reason I prefer to use my left hand and arm in giving my dog the "Sit" signal, rather than the right arm — as used by most handlers, is because it provides more contrast to the other arm signals, thus giving additional aid to the dog.

Probably the most common mistake made by inexperienced Utility handlers is that they make their arm signals too fast. Apparently they feel that a quick movement will have more authority than a slower arm motion. The problem with this theory, however, is that if the dog turns his head for an instant he is likely to miss the signal. Consequently, it is much better to make your arm motions more deliberate. Care should be taken, however, to avoid holding the signals too long, since the Regulations prescribe that the arm must be "promptly returned to a normal position."

Making his signals too fast was one of the problems Fred had to overcome when he began teaching Thunder the Signal Exercise.

Fred started training Thunder for Utility at about the same time he began his Open training, though he took it slower and easier. Each week Fred introduced Thunder to a new Utility exercise, always keeping it "fun and games."

In my opinion, it is even more essential that Utility training be made enjoyable for the dog than it is in the Novice and Open classes. In fact it is critical. There are certain Utility exercises, such as scent discrimination, that *require* a low key, fun and games approach. If you get too tough with him your dog may be too nervous to use his nose; he will pick up the first scent article he comes to and race back with it, in an effort to please you, as I'll get into in more detail in the following chapter. Utility exercises require more *thinking* on the dog's part than anything he had to do in the Novice or Open classes. Thus, I repeat, make Utility training *fun* for your dog. Believe me, in the long run you'll be saving time, as well as having a happier worker than those dogs that have been force trained.

Fortunately for Fred, Thunder learned the Signal Exercise quite easily, with no problems. At first, of course, Fred kept his dog on leash while giving him the hand signals, so that he could enforce the signals. Within two weeks, however, he was able to work Thunder off leash. Fred gradually increased the distance between himself and his dog. Within a month he was able to walk to the opposite end of the yard; Thunder continued to respond obediently to his master's hand signals. Moreover, on the "Come" signal he raced in to the front position with his tail going the entire time.

126

"Heel!"

Your dog's "finish" should be straight, with his shoulder next to your left leg.

By conscientiously avoiding a heavy-handed approach to his training, Fred achieved what we were striving for, a dog that was not only precise but that was obviously a happy worker. From that point on Fred's main problem was to polish his own handling techniques in the Signal Exercise.

In this exercise a surprisingly common handler's error is that in their nervousness some people momentarily forget that they are not allowed to give verbal commands. Further, this "goof" is not restricted to inexperienced handlers. It even happens to the "old pros" occasionally. At a trial a few years ago, for example, one of the best obedience handlers in our area was ready to begin the Signal Exercise. When the judge gave her the order, "Forward," she looked straight at her dog and loudly and clearly sang out, "Perry, heel!" Her face was more than a little red when she came out of the ring.

Another point: Unfortunately, when they reach the Utility class many handlers seem to feel that they no longer have to work on the basic obedience exercises, such as heeling and straight sits, etc. This is a mistake. Just as many, if not more, points are lost for sloppy heeling and crooked sits in the Utility class as in the lower classes. Usually, the difference between being "in the ribbons" and being an "also-ran" can be attributed directly to points lost for these minor infractions. Therefore, in your daily practice sessions it is important that you always include some heeling and other basic routines, insisting on perfection.

Question: At the start of the Utility Signal Exercise the judge ordered, "Forward." Without giving his dog any apparent hand signal the handler started forward. His Shepherd moved forward right along with him, sticking to his handler's left side like a burr.

After a "Halt" order the judge again ordered, "Forward." Once again the dog and handler moved forward together without the handler giving a visible hand signal to his dog. This pattern was repeated consistently on every "Forward" order. Each time the dog heeled perfectly.

On the "Stand," "Down," "Sit," and "Come" portions of the exercise the handler gave his dog the conventional arm signals, the dog completing the exercise almost flawlessly.

The judge failed the dog, on the ground that a "Heel" signal from the handler is mandatory in this exercise. Was the judge correct?

Answer: According to the AKC Regulations, "On order from the judge 'Forward,' the handler *may* signal his dog to walk at heel." Thus, while it is permissible to give a "Heel" signal, it is *not mandatory!* The judge erred.

Question: At the beginning of the Signal Exercise, the handler, in one of those unconscious reflex actions, inadvertently called her dog's name before giving him the signal to heel. She did *not* say, "Rover, heel," she just said "Rover." Realizing immediately what she had done, the handler put her hand over her mouth and gave the signal to heel.

The dog started forward only on the signal, not when his name was called.

The dog performed all parts of the exercise well. Nevertheless the judge failed him, stating that a deduction of more than 50% of the available points was required under the Regulations.

Was the judge correct?

Answer: The Regulations state that a dog must receive a score of zero if the handler gives an audible command to the dog "to stand or remain standing where left, or to drop, or to sit and stay, or to come . . ." However, the rules further recite, "A *substantial deduction* shall be made for any audible command during the *Heeling* or Finish portions of the exercise." Thus, in the case in question, the judge was wrong. The dog should have received a substantial deduction, but *not* a failing score.

An example of a situation where both the dog's name and a hand signal may be used is when you order your dog to "Stay" (in exercises other than the Utility Signal Exercise). In this instance, both a verbal command and simultaneous hand signal are specifically permitted. Therefore, under the Regulations, you may also use the dog's name.

Question: In the Signal Exercise, on the judge's order to "Stand your dog," the middle-aged woman in the ring leaned over and swung her hand in front of the tiny Toy Poodle heeling at her side. The dog halted abruptly and stood at attention like a little soldier.

On the order, "Leave your dog," the handler again leaned over to give her dog the "Stay" signal.

Upon the completion of the exercise, which the eager little Poodle performed excellently, the judge announced to the handler that her dog was a nice worker but that *she* had failed the exercise!

Dumbfounded, the handler asked, "Why?"

"You can't bend your body when giving your dog a hand signal," replied the judge. "When you leaned over to give the 'Stand' and 'Stay' signals you were guilty of a double command."

129

When the woman protested that her dog only stood 8½ inches at the withers, and that she *had* to bend over somewhat in order for the dog to see her signals, the judge curtly replied, "That's too bad, it's one of the disadvantages of having a small dog!"

Diplomacy was obviously not one of this judge's more endearing qualities. But was he correct in his ruling?

Answer: No. The Regulations allow a handler to "bend as far as necessary to bring his hand on a level with his dog's eyes."

Question: In a Utility class at a trial a few years ago a Boxer and a Sheltie were tied for third place. In the Utility class in the event of a tie the dogs must perform at the same time all or some part of the Signal Exercise.

Shortly after the start of the run-off it was apparent that the Sheltie was working well but the Boxer had "fallen apart." It seemed certain the Sheltie had won the run-off.

However, as the two dogs sat in front of their handlers after the signal Recall, it became obvious the Sheltie was not sitting. She was "fouling the ring." The Sheltie not only lost the run-off, but the judge cancelled her previously earned qualifying score.

Can a dog that relieves itself during a run-off lose a previously earned qualifying score?

Answer: The judge "blew it." The Regulations recite that, "The original scores shall not be changed," regardless of a dog's performance in a run-off. Under the circumstances, the Sheltie should have lost the run-off, but should have been placed fourth, with her original, qualifying score.

Scent Discrimination

TRIAL REQUIREMENTS:

The handler shall present all ten scent articles (five leather, five metal) to the judge, who shall select the one leather and one metal article to be used. The handler has the option as to which article, leather or metal, he uses first. The handler's scent may be imparted to the article only with his hands.

Before the start of the exercise the judge or steward will handle each of the remaining eight articles before placing them at random in the ring about 6 inches apart, and about 15 feet from the handler and dog. On order from the judge the handler immediately will place his "scented" article on the judge's book or worksheet and the judge, without touching the article with his hands, will place it among the other articles.

Prior to turning and sending him, the handler may give his scent to the dog by gently touching the dog's nose with the palm of one hand. The dog shall go out to the articles at a brisk pace, though he may take any reasonable time to select the right article providing he works continuously. After picking up the right article the dog shall return at a brisk pace and complete the exercise as in the Retrieve on the Flat.

The same procedure is followed in each of the two scent discrimination exercises.

FAULTS:

Retrieving the wrong article results, of course, in failure. Substantial deductions shall be made for a dog that picks up a wrong article, even though he puts it down again immediately. Minor or substantial deductions, depending on the circumstances in each case, shall be made for a dog that is slow or inattentive, or that does not work continuously.

"Double bar" (or "triple bar") scent articles are not only easier for your dog to pick up, but there is more surface area upon which to place your hand scent.

"Atta boy, that's the right one."

MANY PEOPLE feel that scent discrimination is the most difficult exercise to teach a would-be Utility dog. I disagree. To me, getting a dog to "go out" on the directed jumping exercise is far more of a problem. If a dog is started properly, in my opinion, the Scent Discrimination exercise is not difficult.

I believe in starting a dog's scent discrimination training as early as possible. However, the dog must be far enough along in Open work to have learned to retrieve before he can be taught the Scent Discrimination exercise, which is based upon retrieving.

Fred introduced Thunder to scent discrimination just as soon as his dog had mastered retrieving.

There are a lot of theories and "best methods" advanced by trainers around the country for teaching the Scent Discrimination exercise. However, my favorite, and the method we used with Thunder, is what I call the "hot dog" method.

Get about a dozen ordinary wooden clothespins (wood retains scent better than metal or leather.) Deodorize all of the clothespins by holding them under your kitchen hot water faucet — using tongs of the type you use when cooking corn on the cob. Thus you avoid getting any of your own scent on the clothespins. Place the clean articles in a bucket or other open-top container that allows air to circulate around the articles.

The first day we started teaching Thunder scent discrimination Fred removed one of the clothespins from the bucket. He then proceeded to rub it with a generous portion of hot dog. Next, he threw the clothespin for Thunder, telling him to "Bring it!" Thunder, after sniffing the tasty-smelling clothespin for about a minute, picked it up and returned it to his master, with the help of a little verbal coaxing. Fred rewarded him with a small piece of hot dog.

The same routine was followed for the next two days. Then it was time for the first test.

The next day Fred put "Thunder's clothespin," which was by now thoroughly saturated with both Fred's scent and the irresistible fragrance of hot dog, in his pocket. Using the tongs, he removed one of the clean clothespins from the bucket. He then placed both articles about 15 feet from Thunder, spaced about six inches apart, and told him to "Bring it."

Thunder trotted out to the clothespins. Not surprisingly, he started to pick up the first one he came to, which happened to be the clean one. Fred quickly gave him a firm "No" command. Thunder was confused. So he did what any thinking dog would do — he lay down on both the clothespins, and wagged his tail as though to say, "What the heck am I supposed to do?"

Fred called him back.

Replacing the now not-so-clean clothespin with a fresh, unscented one, Fred repeated the experiment. This time he placed the articles about a foot apart, with the smelly one closer to Thunder. On the command to "Bring it," Thunder again went out and, after glancing back questioningly at his master, he picked up the right pin. With considerable verbal encouragement from Fred, he brought it back. Fred rewarded him with a tasty bit of hot dog.

Now came the more difficult part. Fred placed "Thunder's clothespin" *beyond* the other one.

Upon the command to bring it, Thunder walked somewhat hesitantly out to the first article. He sniffed it for a few seconds. Then, with another backward glance at his young handler, he proceeded to the next one — "his." He sniffed it for a few seconds, picked it up, and brought it back to his master. Fred gave him another tasty reward, plus a *lot* of praise.

The foundation for the Scent Discrimination exercise had now been laid — Thunder had learned that he was not to merely go out and retrieve the first article he came to. He was beginning to realize he must use his nose.

The next day Fred placed two "clean" articles out for Thunder, in addition to "his" clothespin (on which Fred rubbed more hot dog).

Thunder had not forgotten the lesson from the previous day. After sniffing both the "clean" clothespins, he picked up the scented one, and trotted back to his master — again receiving a reward for his efforts.

Gradually, day by day, Fred began putting less and less meat scent on the clothespin to be retrieved and more of his own hand scent. Within three weeks he was able to phase out the hot dog scent entirely. Thunder continued to retrieve the "hand-scented" clothespin, always with a treat for a job well done.

Then it was time to introduce Thunder to the leather scent articles. Fred started with only two articles, a clean one and the "smelly one." No problem.

Day by day Fred introduced more "clean" articles to the group, until he was using all five leather articles. Occasionally Thunder goofed, picking up the wrong article, but Fred didn't lose his patience (which is absolutely *essential* in this exercise). Within two weeks Thunder was retrieving the right article consistently.

134

Thunder receives a treat for retrieving the right article.

The metal articles presented more of a problem. Metal doesn't retain scent as well as leather or wood and most dogs are reluctant to pick up a metal object; they don't like the feel on their teeth. However, by starting over again, with only two articles — a clean one and a scented one, Fred succeeded in less than a week in teaching Thunder to retrieve the proper metal article.

Combining the leather and metal scent articles did not present too much of a problem. By that time Thunder knew what was expected of him, and he complied happily, always anticipating a tasty reward.

Thunder's main problem in the Scent Discrimination exercise was that while he performed well in his own backyard, where there was relatively little distraction, when he was called upon to perform the exercise in a strange locale, at an exhibition or fun match, for example, he seemed to fall apart. He acted as though he had never done the exercise before. To remedy this, Fred practiced with Thunder at various locations — a local college campus, a shopping center parking lot, etc. But it took about six months before Thunder was 100% reliable in any location other than his own yard.

With respect to the best type of scent articles, the AKC Regulations permit you to use ". . . two sets, each comprised of five identical articles not more than six inches in length, which may be items of every-day use. One set shall be made entirely of rigid metal, and one of leather of such design that nothing but leather is visible. . . The articles must be legibly numbered. . ." In other words, the articles do not have to be of any specific shape or design; in fact, some handlers use metal salt shakers and other common household items. This is all right so long as all of the articles in each set are identical, and legibly numbered. In addition, the leather articles must be so constructed that nothing but leather is visible except for the minimum amount of thread or metal necessary to hold the article together.

For those of you who, like the writer, are all thumbs when it comes to making things, it would be wise to buy a commercial set of regulation scent articles. A good set can be purchased for less than $40. They will last for many years if properly cared for. Moreover, professionally designed dumbbell-type scent articles are easier for a dog to pick up, particularly the so-called "double bar" style articles.

To clean your scent articles, there are several methods which can be used. Some handlers use a light solution of disinfectant or mild soap suds, while others soak their articles in boiling water. Personally, however, I don't believe either is necessary. Further, washing in hot water will soon ruin your leather articles.

In the early training stages it is advisable to wash your scent articles after each use, but this can be accomplished merely by holding them under the cold water faucet for ten or fifteen seconds, rather than washing them in hot water, or with soap. After your dog has mastered the exercise it should be necessary merely to allow the air to deodorize the articles between training sessions. However, it's definitely a good idea at least to rinse your scent articles prior to a trial.

When imparting your hand scent to your dog before "sending" him, the Regulations state that you may touch the dog's nose with the palm of your hand to give him your scent. However, this does not mean that you should rub your hand all over his face. Not only is this contrary to the intent of the rule, but his nostrils are likely to become so saturated with your scent that he can't smell anything else when he gets out to the articles, with the result that all of the articles will smell like you to him.

With Thunder, we found that he had a tendency to turn his head away when Fred attempted to place his hand over Thunder's nose. Inasmuch as Thunder was well familiar with Fred's hand scent, we discovered that Thunder performed better without this aid. It has been my experience that this is true of many dogs. If your dog is one of those that does not particularly enjoy having his nose covered with your hand, forget it. It isn't necessary — your dog knows your scent.

136

Question: Before starting the Scent Discrimination exercise, the judge made the handler turn his back to the unscented articles as they were being placed in the ring by the steward.

The handler, somewhat disgruntled, told the judge that this was contrary to the Regulations.

Was the judge correct in his ruling, and, if not, what recourse did the handler have?

Answer: The AKC Regulations state, "Handler and dog shall turn around *after* watching the judge or steward spread the articles . . . ." Thus, the judge was wrong.

A ruling by a judge which is obviously contrary to the Obedience Regulations should definitely be reported both to the trial committee and the AKC. If the judge was wrong he will hear from the AKC. Moreover, if there are too many such legitimate complaints filed against a particular judge, the AKC has the power to withdraw that individual's approval as an obedience judge. I know of one situation in which a judge was "asked to resign."

Question: In the Scent Discrimination exercise, while the dog was working over the articles, smelling each one, he accidentally knocked another article on top of the scented one. The dog picked up and brought back *both* articles. The judge failed the dog.

Was the judge's ruling proper?

Answer: The Regulations are clear on this point, the dog must be failed! The Regulations state: " . . . a dog that *retrieves a wrong article* must be marked zero for the particular exercise."

Question: One of my favorite stories concerning "incidents" that have occurred in obedience rings is the following:

At a large obedience trial, with split "A" and "B" Utility classes, both classes were being judged simultaneously in roped-off rings that abutted each other. In one ring the judge was putting a Doberman through the Directed Retrieve exercises. At the near end of the adjoining ring a woman handler was about to start the Scent Discrimination exercise with her Golden Retriever.

As the woman stood with her back to her ring, rubbing her hand scent on the first article, the Golden sat at her side looking under the rope, intently watching the proceedings in the adjacent ring.

The Dobe's judge gave the handler the order, "The glove on your left."

With a perplexed expression on his face the handler said, "Send my dog after what? The Golden from the next ring *just took the glove!*"

What happened was that the Golden carefully marked the spot where the closest glove lay in the adjoining ring. Then, when his mistress ordered him to "Get it," meaning the first scent article, the Golden dashed under the ring rope into the next ring and retrieved the glove, sitting in front of his handler with the glove in his mouth and his tail wagging a mile a minute, as if to say, "Ain't I the greatest!"

After she got over her initial shock, the Golden's handler shrugged and joined in the laughter of the crowd.

If you were the judge in the Golden's ring, what would you have done?

Before you answer, remember the Regulations specify, "If a dog has failed in a particular part of an exercise, it shall not ordinarily be rejudged nor given a second chance; *but* if in the judge's opinion the dog's performance was prejudiced by *peculiar* and *unusual conditions,* the judge may at his own discretion rejudge the dog on the entire exercise."

Would you, as the judge, have given the Golden another chance to do the Scent Discrimination exercise?

Answer: Had I been the judge, I would have failed the dog, despite the fact that I would have felt very sorry for his handler. In my personal opinion, dogs performing in an adjacent ring do not constitute such a "peculiar and unusual condition" as is required in order to justify the rejudging of a dog. This condition exists at almost every trial. In addition, I believe that giving the Golden a second chance would be unfair to the other dogs in the class that passed despite distractions (and did not "leave the ring," which is *verboten.*)

The Directed Retrieve Exercise

TRIAL REQUIREMENTS:

In this exercise the handler stands with his dog sitting at the heel position, midway between the two jumps. The handler will provide three predominantly white cotton work gloves, which the judge or steward shall place at the end of the ring, one in each corner and one in the center, about three feet from the end and/or side of the ring.

The judge will give the order, "One," "Two," or "Three," reading from left to right. The handler must give the command to heel and turn with his dog to face the designated glove. He may not turn completely around nor touch his dog to get him in position.

The handler will then give his dog the direction to the designated glove with a single motion of his left hand and arm, and the command to retrieve. The dog shall go directly to the glove, and retrieve it, at a brisk pace, completing the exercise as in the Retrieve On the Flat.

The handler may bend his knees and body in giving the direction to the dog and in giving the command to retrieve, after which the handler will stand erect with his arms at his sides. The exercise shall consist of a single retrieve, but the judge shall designate different glove positions for successive dogs.

FAULTS:

A dog that fails to go out on a single command, that does not go directly to the designated glove, or that fails to retrieve the glove must be marked zero. Similarly, a dog that anticipates his handler's command to retrieve, or that does not return promptly with the glove sufficiently close so that the handler can readily take it

Introduce your dog to the gloves by throwing one to retrieve. (Don't spare praise.)

Start with short retrieves, with wide angles.

"What's so tough about this?"

without moving either foot or stretching forward must be failed. Depending upon the specific circumstances, minor or substantial deductions shall be made for: a handler who over-turns, for touching the dog or for excessive movements in getting him to heel facing the designated glove. All other deductions listed under Retrieve On the Flat shall also apply.

THE DIRECTED RETRIEVE is far more difficult to teach a dog than it may at first appear.

The first thing, of course, is to introduce your dog to the gloves. Throw one for him to retrieve, so that he becomes accustomed to picking up and returning the glove to you. With most Open-trained dogs this can be accomplished in one throw.

The main problem in the Directed Retrieve exercise is getting the dog to retrieve the glove you are pointing to when all three gloves are visible to him. All too frequently a dog will want to retrieve the first glove that catches his eye. It may or may not be the designated glove. Your task is to get the dog to sight along your arm, so that his attention is directed to the proper glove. This takes time, practice, and patience.

Initially, to make it easier for your dog, spread the gloves out in a line only about seven or eight feet in front of the dog. Thus, when you pivot to send him after one of the side gloves, the angle is much greater than when he is back twenty or more feet from the gloves, as he will be in the ring. This greater angle has the same effect as placing the gloves further apart. It makes it easier for the dog to recognize which glove you wish him to retrieve.

Take this exercise slow and easy. Don't rush it.

After your dog is consistently retrieving the proper glove from a distance of seven or eight feet from the line of the gloves you can gradually, week by week, begin increasing the distance from the gloves before sending him. Thus you decrease the angle of his pivot and increase the difficulty of the exercise. However, it will probably be many, many weeks before he is ready to retrieve from the full distance. Even then he will occasionally goof. It will be months (if ever) before you will be fully confident of your dog in this exercise.

Another tip which may be helpful in the early stages of teaching your dog the Directed Retrieve is to exaggerate your pivot when getting him in position to retrieve either of the side gloves. Turn approximately 90 degrees. Then there can be little mistake as to which glove you wish him to retrieve. However, as your dog improves, gradually reduce the degree of your turn so that, eventually, you pivot only far enough to position him facing directly toward the designated glove. This is the limit you may turn in the ring. In fact, in a trial the dog must be able to see all three gloves when the handler turns to face the glove designated by the judge.

When pivoting to face the designated glove you may give your dog a verbal command (*not* a signal) to "Heel," but you may not touch him. Nor may you take a step forward or back while pivoting. This is a common handler's error. You must pivot *in place*.

Another thing in this exercise, you may not pump your arm back and forth several times when giving your dog the direction. You must give him the direction to the designated glove with a *single* motion of your *left* arm and hand along the right side of the dog, while giving the verbal command to retrieve either simultaneously with or immediately following the arm signal. Under the revised Regulations, if you have a small dog you may bend your knees and body to align your arm with his head, *without* a deduction.

Regarding the question, incidentally, of what is a "substantial" deduction, as opposed to a "minor" deduction, I have been queried on this point many times. This is strictly a discretionary matter with each judge. However, I believe you will find that the majority of obedience judges abide fairly closely to the following rule of thumb: a substantial deduction is two and a half points or greater, while a minor deduction is from one-half to two points.

Questions: Are white work gloves with colored cuffs acceptable in the Directed Retrieve exercise? How about nylon work gloves, or hard-backed leather work gloves with canvas palms?

Answer: A colored cuff is permissible, as it is still a *predominantly* white work glove. Nylon work gloves or combination leather and canvas gloves are *not* acceptable. The gloves must be standard cotton work gloves (not gauntlet).

Question: How should a judge score a small dog that necessarily drags the glove on the floor while retrieving it?

Answer: If a little dog has to drag the glove back he will *not* be penalized. A dog need not lift the glove completely clear of the floor.

Directed Jumping

TRIAL REQUIREMENTS:

The handler, from a position on the center line of the ring and about 20 feet from the line of the jumps, shall stand with his dog sitting in the heel position. On order from the judge the handler shall command and/or signal his dog to go forward at a brisk pace to a point about 20 feet beyond the jumps, and in the approximate center. When the dog has reached this point the handler shall give him a command to sit. The dog must stop and sit with his attention on the handler. The judge will designate which jump (high jump or bar jump) is to be taken first by the dog, and the handler shall command and/or signal the dog to return to him over the designated jump. While the dog is in mid-air the handler may turn so as to be facing the dog as he returns. The dog shall sit in front of the handler and, on order from the judge, finish as in the Recall.

When the dog is again sitting in the heel position the judge shall ask, "Are you ready?" before giving the order to send the dog for the second part of the exercise. The same procedure shall be followed for second jump.

FAULTS:

A dog must receive a score of zero for the following: anticipating the handler's command and/or signal to go out, not leaving the handler, not going at least 10 feet beyond the jumps, not stopping on command, anticipating the handler's command and/or signal to jump, not jumping as directed, knocking the bar off the uprights, climbing or using the top of the high jump for aid in going over.

Substantial deductions shall be made for a dog that turns, stops, or sits before the handler's command to sit, and for a dog that fails to sit. Substantial or minor deductions, depending on the extent, shall be made for slowness in going out or for touching the jumps. All of the penalties listed under Recall shall also apply.

A diagonal bar or rod helps deter a dog from running *under* the bar jump.

"Thunder, fetch it!" (Keep the bar low, at first.)

FOR MANY PEOPLE, the most difficult part of the Directed Jumping exercise is teaching their dogs to jump the bar jump, rather than run under it — which is quite a temptation.

I introduce our dogs to the bar jump early, just as soon as they have mastered the Open Retrieve Over the High Jump. At that point I start them retrieving over the bar jump, with the bar set *very* low. I also place a rod or bar diagonally spanning the upright supports beneath the bar, extending upwardly from the ground adjacent one support to the opposite support (see photo). This gives the visual impression that it is not just open space beneath the bar; it tends to deter the dog from running *under* the bar.

If your dog is eagerly retrieving over the solid jump the transition to the bar jump should not be too difficult.

At the start, position your dog close to the *low* bar jump. Tease him with his dumbbell. Then, while he is excited and anxious to chase it, toss the dumbbell a *short* distance over the jump. Usually, in his eagerness to retrieve his dumbbell the dog will sail over the bar before he even realizes what he is doing.

The real trick is to get your dog to *return over the jump,* rather than under or around it. To accomplish this, as soon as he takes off in quest of his dumbbell quickly step forward to a position where you can pat the top of the bar, encouraging him to "jump" just as soon as he picks up the dumbbell. Your first few tries will probably not be successful; the chances are that your dog will return *around* the jump. This was the problem Fred encountered with Thunder in the early stages of Thunder's Directed Jumping training. However, if you keep your throws short, your dog should be returning over the bar after a few days. When he does, *lavish* him with praise!

Your dog may be one of those rascals that goes over the bar on the way out, but persists in returning *around* the jump. To cure this, set up lawn chairs or other "barriers" at the opposite sides of the jump. If he remembers his geometry, Prince will quickly realize that the shortest distance between two points is a straight line. If he wants his praise and/or tidbit he will soon start returning over the bar, rather than around the jump. Once this is accomplished, he should be taking the jump in both directions consistently within a week. The "barriers" can then be removed. And the bar can be gradually raised, week by week. Also, the rod or other diagonal obstruction can be withdrawn. However, it should be replaced immediately if your dog starts running under the bar.

By thus introducing your dog to the bar jump while he is still working on his Open exercises it will be old hat to him by the time he reaches Utility.

While the bar jump presents a problem for many dogs, as I mentioned, in my opinion the more difficult part of teaching a dog the Directed Jumping exercise is getting him to "go out" or "advance" properly. I also start teaching my dogs this portion of the exercise long before they are ready for Utility.

Initially, I place a handkerchief, or other plainly visible "target," about 60 feet from the dog. I then run him out to the target and let him watch me place a tasty goodie (or his favorite toy) on the target. We then run back to the starting position and I have him sit at heel, facing the target (while I regain my breath.) It is important that the dog learn right from the beginning that a "brisk pace" is required in this exercise.

The next step is to give the dog an enthusiastic verbal command to "Advance" (or whatever term you prefer) while simultaneously giving him a pumping hand motion with your left hand. The dog is apt to be confused the first few times; it might be necessary for you to run out to the target with him. Once he reaches the target let him eat the goodie. Praise him. Then have him sit and stay, while you return to the starting place.

Next, call your dog in to the front position. In a few sessions he will get the idea that this is a "fun" exercise. Before too long he will be racing out to the target on command; it won't be necessary for you to run out with him.

When your dog is performing the above step consistently it is time to begin reducing the size of the target. If you are using a handkerchief or piece of white paper as a target, fold it in half. In a few days fold it again, gradually, day by day, reducing the size of the target until eventually it will be barely visible to your dog. By this time he should be automatically advancing straight out, in quest of his tidbit or toy. You can then remove both the target and treat. The "advance" will be so deeply instilled in your dog that he will continue to respond to your command. However, it is a good idea to occasionally place a treat out for him, in order to maintain his zest and enthusiasm.

By following the steps outlined above, when your dog reaches the Utility Class he will already have learned the basics of the Directed Jumping exercise. Putting it all together is relatively easy.

First, have your dog "go out" in a line between the jumps, which should be set low. When he reaches the opposite end of the yard call his name; as he turns to face you tell him to "Sit." (The straightness of his sit is of no import in a trial.) Then move over to a position directly behind one of the jumps. Call your dog "Over," while simultaneously

"Good boy, over!"

Thunder retrieves over the bar set at the full height he will be required to jump in trials.

"How does that tidbit look, big boy?"

Ready, set . . . "Advance!"

"Over!"

swinging your arm upwardly to a horizontal position. (Left jump, left arm, etc.) As your dog begins his leap, quickly back-pedal to a position centered between the jumps, calling your dog into the front position. Have him "finish," and pour on the praise. Repeat this procedure with the other jump.

When calling your dog over the jump it may be necessary for you to move up and pat the top of the jump, thus lending encouragement and emphasis to your command.

Once your dog has the idea, you can *gradually* begin positioning yourself further from the jump, and closer to the center line, when commanding him to take the jump. Eventually you will be able to remain in a centered position and send him over the designated jump merely by raising your arm and verbally ordering him, "Over." However, don't rush it. *And* keep the jumps low until your dog is 100% reliable in the exercise. When he reaches this point you can gradually increase the height of the jumps until he is ultimately clearing the height he will be required to jump in trials.

Some of you may be wondering why I start a dog out advancing at least 60 feet when introducing him to the Directed Jumping exercise, which is further than he will have to advance in the ring. A number of obedience instructors begin having the dog advance only 10 or 15 feet, gradually increasing the distance as he progresses. However, you will notice that the majority of dogs that fail this exercise in trials do so because they don't advance far enough, thus leaving themselves too sharp an angle to the jumps. This can be particularly disastrous at indoor trials, where the floor is likely to be slippery. The dog will have a problem if he doesn't advance far enough to align himself with the matting leading diagonally to the jumps. However, you can always stop a trained dog's advance when he reaches the proper spot merely by calling his name and telling him to sit. On the other hand, if your dog turns and sits without going out far enough you are in trouble.

It is for this reason that I believe in teaching a dog to advance further than is required in trials right from the start of his Directed Jumping training. I don't want him to get the idea that a short advance is *ever* allowable.

Another point which I should perhaps elaborate upon is the proper arm signal to be used when directing your dog over the designated jump. According to the AKC Regulations, after giving your dog an arm signal, ". . . . the arm must immediately be returned to a natural position." This means, of course, that you cannot stand there interminably looking like a one-armed scarecrow. However, if your dog should momentarily glance away just as you are giving the signal continue holding your arm outstretched until he sees it. A substantial deduction is better than failure.

The Regulations also require that the handler face straight ahead while giving his dog the signal indicating the designated jump. However, as stated in the rules, "While the dog is in mid-air the handler *may* turn so as to be facing the dog as it returns."

Question: A dog goes out about 8 feet beyond the jumps. The handler gives the command to sit only after it is evident that the dog is about to sit anyway. The dog takes the jump as directed.

Would you, as the judge, pass such a performance?

Answer: If a dog anticipates the sit command he should receive a substantial deduction for his error. However, in the situation described, the dog must receive a zero for the exercise because of his failure to go out "at least 10 feet beyond the jumps," as specified in the Regulations.

Question: Thus far the not-so-young Basset Hound in the ring has passed every exercise; he is within a whisker of earning his first leg on that elusive U.D. title.

On the judge's order to "Send your dog," the handler tells her dog to "Go out," the Basset advancing nicely to the opposite end of the ring. (Not setting any speed records, but straight.) As his handler calls out, "Flash, sit!" the dog stops and turns to face her, but instead of sitting Flash continues to *stand,* looking at his mistress with innocent, soulful eyes.

After waiting a reasonable length of time for the dog to sit, the judge finally orders, "The bar jump," whereupon Flash completes the first half of the exercise without any further innovations of his own.

In the second half of the exercise the Basset does everything correctly.

How should Flash be scored?

Answer: If you said the dog must be failed because of his failure to sit on command—you are wrong! The refusal of a dog to sit on command in this exercise calls for a "substantial deduction," but *not* failure.

The Group Examination

THE EASIEST of the Utility exercises is the Group Exam. At least it should be, inasmuch as the dogs have been standing for examination since their early Novice training days. Certainly by the time he reaches the Utility class a dog should be steady while being examined, showing no shyness or resentment.

The most difficult part of this exercise is getting your dog used to standing, without shifting his feet, for as long as five minutes.

The Regulations specify that the handlers must have been away from their dogs for *at least three minutes* before the judge's order, "Back to your dogs." As a practical matter, however, if it is a large Utility class with a full complement of 15 dogs in the group, or close to it, it will probably be more like five minutes before the judge completes his examination of all the dogs. Therefore, in your practice sessions it is advisable to have your dog stand for five minutes, or longer. In addition, whenever possible have various people examine your dog, both men and women — so that the dog will become accustomed to being examined by "judges" of either sex. If you are a member of a training class this should be no problem; if not, you will have to rely on neighbors or visiting friends.

The mistake many inexperienced handlers make in this exercise is that they don't set their dogs up properly at the beginning of the exercise. As a result, their dogs may be standing in an awkward or uncomfortable position. More than likely they will shift position before the exercise is over. But under the Regulations, you are allowed to pose your dog. Therefore, be sure that your dog is standing squarely, and is comfortable, before you leave him.

While the Group Exam exercise should not be too difficult to teach your dog, it is important that you practice it at home — if not every day, at *least* three times a week.

Make sure your dog is standing squarely, and is comfortable, before leaving him.

Push down slightly on his rump to signal your dog that this is the Long Stand (a legitimate "extra command").

Although Thunder had never given Fred any problem in the Novice Stand for Exam, the Utility exam proved far more of a test. In his early Utility training, Thunder got restless after about two minutes and would move his feet slightly to shift his weight to a new position. It took many months before Thunder was 100% reliable for a full five minutes. And this was the result of *daily* practice sessions.

I recall the dialogue Fred and I had at the conclusion of almost every practice session:

"Let's skip the Stand for Exam today, Dad. Thunder knows that."

"O.K., wise guy, I'll bet you a nickel he can't stand still for five minutes without shifting his feet."

I lost quite a few nickels, but at least I accomplished my objective — Fred and Thunder practiced the exercise. (Besides, I took the money out of Sally's cookie jar.)

After their dogs reach the Utility class, too many handlers feel that they no longer have to spend much time on the so-called "easy" exercises, heeling and straight sits, etc. This is a mistake. Just as many points are usually lost for sloppy heeling and crooked sits in the Utility class as in the lower classes. Frequently, the difference between being a winner and being out of the ribbons is the result of points lost for these minor infractions. Therefore, as I have tried to emphasize not only in this section but also in the section on Open training, in your daily practice sessions it is *critical* that you include some heeling and other basic routines, always *insisting* upon perfection.

Before getting into the story of Thunder's trials and tribulations in Utility-land, there is something I'd like to get off my chest.

Over the past decade obedience trials have not only grown terrifically in number and size, but the quality of the dogs' performances has also improved greatly. Performances that won first place a few years ago would not even be good enough to place in many of today's trials. Moreover, today's judges have "sharper pencils" than ever before; they have to, in order to distinguish among the many top-notch dogs competing. Despite the progress of the sport and improvement in the work of the dogs, however, there is one area in which I'm afraid some of the two-legged competitors have not kept pace — that is sportsmanship.

With the stiffer competition for trophies, some handlers have become so intent on winning that they forget the rules of good sportsmanship when their dogs fail to place. They grumble about everything, from the judging to the weather. They use every excuse in the book.

How many times have we all heard the old saw, "I would have had a 199, but . . ." These people wouldn't dream of congratulating the winner.

Another sad situation that is apparent in today's obedience rings is that in their all-out attempt to win trophies a few handlers are using overly-severe training methods. The result is frightened, slinking dogs that have no zest for their work. The entire time they are in the ring these dogs have their heads lowered and their tails between their legs. Although they may perform the exercises with mechanical perfection they are a poor advertisement for obedience.

One of the principal objects of our sport is to demonstrate to the public not only the ability of a dog to learn and perform obedience exercises, but to perform them willingly. Our dogs should exhibit the self-assurance and cheerful attitude that mark a well-adjusted pet and companion. Further, this is ignored by too many obedience judges, though specifically set forth in the Obedience Regulations, which state that lack of willingness or enjoyment on the part of the dog *must* be penalized.

To me, one of the most heart-warming sights is a dog that performs in the ring with his tail going, his head high, and with his eyes happily riveted on his master in eager anticipation of doing his bidding. This is the type of obedience-trained dog that will win friends and new participants for our sport.

Thunder Over Dixie, U.D.

DESPITE the fact that we didn't feel Thunder was quite ready for Utility competition, we decided to test him in a trial. In his daily practice sessions Thunder was performing fairly well, but he was not consistent. Like the little girl with the curl, when he was good he was very good, but when he was bad — he was horrible.

What the young Shepherd needed was practice under trial conditions, so that we could see where he needed more work. Unfortunately, as I have mentioned before, our area has very few "matches." Thus we had little choice; we entered Thunder in a licensed trial in Jacksonville.

In addition to the fact that the Jacksonville club always runs an excellent trial, the Utility judge was to be "Mr. Obedience," Bob Self. It had been several years since I had seen Bob. I was looking forward to swapping lies with him again.

On the day of the trial we got up before the rooster, arriving in Jacksonville about an hour before the Utility class was scheduled to start. We welcomed the steaming coffee provided by the club's hospitality committee. And, we had an opportunity to chat with Bob.

When the Utility class started Fred and Thunder found a position adjacent the ring, where Fred could study the pattern (while Thunder studied the pretty Golden bitch lying nearby.)

I don't know whether he realized that we weren't expecting too much of him in this, his first Utility trial (which he would consider a personal affront), or whether he was showing off for his new-found lady friend, but Thunder strutted through the first four individual exercises as though he had been doing them all his life.

155

Then came the Directed Jumping exercise.

On Fred's command to "Advance," Thunder jauntily trotted straight out between the jumps. Then, apparently so that the Golden would have a better view of him, he suddenly veered off to the left (which he *never* did in practice.) As he sat, Romeo struck his most elegant pose, full profile.

Fortunately, the first jump was the high jump, the one closest to him. Thunder cleared the jump by at least four inches (which I thought was an unnecessary bit of ostentation). But the damage had been done; his unique advance had cost Thunder valuable points.

Watching from ringside, I knew Fred was dying a thousand deaths — what if Lover Boy pulled the same thing in the second half of the exercise? To get in position to take the bar jump Thunder would have to cross practically the entire width of the ring, over a slippery portion of the floor. And the bar jump had never been Thunder's long suit.

"Send your dog," ordered His Honor.

Sure enough, Thunder did it again. He veered off to the left, closer to his admiring friend.

"The bar jump!"

On Fred's command to jump, Thunder stole a glance at the Golden, then trotted nonchalantly toward the mat leading to the bar jump. Gathering speed as he approached, he sailed over the bar with ease and finished the exercise in the standard manner. Fred looked pale; Thunder looked pompous.

Thunder made it through the Group Exam without incident or innovation.

Curiously, Bob didn't give Thunder any extra credit for his romantic showmanship. Thunder scored 190½, good for second place (1st place was 191). We were pleased, of course, but on the way home from Jacksonville Fred explained to Thunder that there is a time and place for everything; he made it clear that an obedience ring is not the proper place to perform his courting ritual.

After Thunder's unexpectedly satisfactory showing in his first Utility trial we quickly entered him in two upcoming trials — hoping to get his U.D. title before the winter suspension of trials in the area. If he didn't earn his U.D. in the next two trials, Thunder would have to wait five months to try again.

The next trial was in Columbia, S.C., and the following day a trial in Spartanburg, S.C.

At Columbia, Thunder almost caused Fred to suffer a cardiac arrest. In the Scent Discrimination exercise Thunder picked up the wrong metal article, and started back with it. After three or four steps, however, Thunder suddenly had second thoughts. He rudely spit out the article, did an about face, and returned to the group of articles. After about 30 seconds of agonizing investigation of each article in the group he finally selected the right one, dutifully returning with it to his young master. However, his deviation from the ideal performance obviously cost Thunder a substantial deduction.

Nor was the rest of Thunder's performance particularly praiseworthy. In fact, it was downright sloppy.

His score was 184½. However, only two dogs passed, so Thunder again won 2nd place.

The first place dog was the famous Border Collie, Rex, with a score of 199½. (Frankly, I didn't see where he lost the ½ point.)

Describing the placings another way: Thunder took 2nd place among the qualifiers, while the renowned Rex was second from last.

At Spartanburg the following day Thunder really did himself proud. Not only did he retrieve the wrong metal scent article, but in the Signal Exercise he chose the exact moment Fred was giving him the "down" hand signal to turn his head to watch something more interesting in the next ring. He missed the signal completely. But it didn't matter, he had already blown his U.D., at least for the time being.

Although we were pleased that Thunder had earned two legs toward his U.D. title, in his first three trials, we were a little disappointed. He would have to wait until Spring for his next opportunity to gain that all-important third leg.

Thunder Tries Again

The first trial of the Spring season was in Atlanta. This trial, run by the Atlanta Obedience Club, celebrated the club's 25th anniversary. Exhibitors came from as far away as Miami. The quality of the dog's performance was top-notch. The competition was fierce in all classes. As for the facilities, however, I was under-whelmed.

The indoor rings were adequate, but the Utility class was held out-doors, on hard pavement — with no rubber matting to cushion the landing when a dog sailed over a jump.

The trial committee was also negligent in that it hadn't made plans for a tornado the following day. The twister hit Atlanta just as we were preparing to leave for the long drive home.

It was fortunate, of course, that the tornado didn't strike the day before — especially for the Utility entrants. For according to the premium list, the Utility class was to be judged "outdoors *regardless of weather.*"

In view of this experience I think the Atlanta club might wish to modify the wording in its premium list in the future.

Thunder sails over the bar jump.

After a five month absence from the ring Thunder was rusty. During the winter we had neglected his training. However, as soon as we received the Atlanta premium list Fred got off his tail. He put his dog through a rigorous six-week crash program, in an attempt to get Thunder back into trial form.

As the trial date drew nearer the dog began to improve. The week before the trial he looked pretty good; he was scoring in the 190's in his daily workouts. We set out for Atlanta with high hopes.

The Utility class started at one o'clock in the afternoon. Thunder was the seventh dog to go into the ring. Of the first six dogs, only two passed. Was it an omen?

In the first exercise, the Signal Exercise, Thunder lost points for a tardy response to the "down" signal, but he passed.

The Scent Discrimination exercise didn't prove a problem, except for a crooked front and Thunder's returns could have been faster. But, though losing a few points, he again passed. He was one step closer to that coveted U.D. title.

Thoroughly warmed up, Thunder retrieved the proper glove with gusto. In the first half of the Directed Jumping exercise he advanced perfectly, and returned over the high jump with ease.

Now it was time for Thunder's nemesis, the bar jump — the final part of the individual exercises.

Upon Fred's command to "Advance," Thunder trotted regally to the opposite end of the ring. He turned and sat, on command.

"Here it comes." I thought. I knew Fred's heart was in his throat.

The judge said, "The bar jump."

Giving Thunder a menacing look, Fred swung his arm upwardly and ordered, "Over."

Thunder nonchalantly trotted up to the bar, and cleared it by no less than six inches (see photo), returning to the front position and "finishing" smartly. Now, if he could get through the Group Exam, Thunder would have his U.D.

I couldn't watch this final exercise. My nerves were frayed. I retired to the car for a sip of Gatorade.

A short time later Fred and Thunder approached the car. I couldn't tell anything from the expression on the boy's face.

"Well," I asked, "how'd he do?"

"193," Fred answered, a little too casually. "He's a big shot now, a full-fledged Utility Dog."

I let out a sigh of relief; the goal we had set more than two years earlier had been achieved.